POLESDEN LACEY

The playwright Richard Brinsley Sheridan, Polesden Lacey's most famous inhabitant, described it as 'the nicest place, within a prudent distance of town, in England'. The 210,000 people who visit each year find a pastoral oasis that feels much more than 25 miles from central London. That Polesden should have survived since the Middle Ages as a small self-contained agricultural estate is remarkable within such close proximity to the capital. Its preservation is due to the generosity of Mrs Ronald Greville, a legendary Edwardian hostess whose posthumous wish was that Polesden should be 'open to the public at all times' and should be enjoyed by the 'largest number of people'.

Mrs Greville bequeathed Polesden, her London house in Charles Street, Mayfair, and her art collections, with an endowment, to the National Trust in 1942. The bequest was in memory of her father, William McEwan, an Edinburgh brewing millionaire and philanthropist, whose important collection of Dutch Old Masters and other paintings she inherited and augmented on a grand scale, arranging them in surroundings of the utmost opulence. She also bought Italian maiolica, and English, European and Chinese porcelain, silver, bronzes and furniture.

Polesden was purchased by Mrs Greville and her husband in 1906, and was converted by Mewès and Davis, the architects of the newly built Ritz Hotel, into a house fit for royalty. Edward VII stayed for the first time in 1909, a year after the premature death of his close friend Ronald Greville, occupying the King's Suite, which was richly appointed with modern conveniences then rare in country houses. The windows look southwards across the wooded valley towards Ranmore and eastwards over spacious lawns towards Sheridan's rose garden, extended by Mrs Greville and equipped with pergolas, hothouses and every contrivance of modern horticulture. Beyond the walled gardens lay huge beds of vegetables, and Polesden was also self-sufficient in meat and dairy produce, supplies being regularly sent up to Mayfair during the London season to fuel Mrs Greville's lavish entertainments. Her cuisine was renowned even in that age of culinary extravagance and discrimination, and the elaborate menus survive together with lists of Mrs Greville's distinguished and often exotic guests.

Mrs Greville was most famous as a collector of royalties. Her friendship with Edward VII (who thought her 'gift for hospitality' amounted to 'positive genius') inaugurated a lifelong devotion to the House of Windsor. She was especially fond of Queen Mary (consort of George V) and of Queen Elizabeth the Queen Mother, part of whose honeymoon was spent at Polesden in 1923, and whom the childless Mrs Greville loved like a daughter. Mrs Greville was adored by her friends and feared by her rivals for her indiscreet and acerbic wit. In the mid-1930s she became notorious for her reception of Joachim von Ribbentrop, Hitler's special ambassador, but her pro-Nazi stance was, at least to her, not inconsistent with strong patriotism. She died in the Dorchester Hotel in 1942, defiantly refusing to move from her suite during air raids.

After her death, Polesden was rearranged for public opening, but in the process many of the secondary and almost all of the bedroom furnishings were sold in 1943. There was a serious fire in 1960, and although nothing was lost, the original decoration of several rooms was damaged and had to be replaced. In 1995, after extensive research, the Trust embarked upon the restoration and rearrangement of the principal rooms, in order to make their original style and luxury more evident.

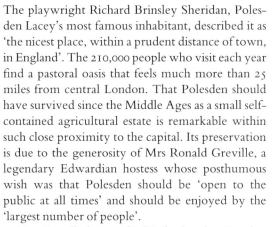

(Left) Huge Chinese famille rose *vases, c.1760, fill the window alcoves in the southern arm of the Picture Corridor*

TOUR OF THE HOUSE

The Exterior

THE EAST (ENTRANCE) FRONT

Since at least 1631, this has been the entrance front, an orientation maintained in successive rebuildings of the house. The present façade was designed and built in 1902–5 by Ambrose Poynter, and remains unaltered apart from the extension of the left-hand wing by Mrs Greville's architects, Mewès and Davis, in about 1906–9. Concurrently, to make the range symmetrical, they added a matching semicircular bow front to the right-hand wing, which has blind windows on the ground floor (to mask the kitchen behind). Flanking bow fronts were something of a Mewès and Davis trademark, having already appeared on a grander scale at Luton Hoo in Bedfordshire (1903–7). The yellow colour wash on the stucco, the white-painted windows and cement dressings remain as originally intended by Poynter. Early in his career he had won a competition for a clock-tower in Buenos Aires, which may partly explain the inclusion of one here as a much-needed vertical accent. He also designed the curious tall covered chimneystacks.

The limestone well-head is Venetian, *c.*1380, and was moved here after 1948. A columnar sundial, now in the walled garden, was Mrs Greville's original centrepiece. The marble flight of steps, flanked by lead putti on stone pedestals, was moved 60 yards northwards from its original position in the centre of the bank opposite the front door by 1933–6.

THE SOUTH FRONT

The principal façade of the house faced east, but since the additions of 1735–48 the south front has assumed an equal, if not greater, importance in order to take advantage of the sunshine and of the magnificent views across the valley towards Ranmore. The middle six bays with the central

Ionic portico survive from Thomas Cubitt's villa of 1821–3. Poynter added a central pediment and an extra bay at either end in 1903–5. He also intended the south front, when seen from a distance, to gain in grandeur by being flanked by the set-back wings to the north. The two end bays on the right-hand side were added by Mewès and Davis *c.*1906–9. They also introduced the massive flanking urns on the terrace, and the pair of griffins at the head of the central steps (which they converted from two flights into one). In Mrs Greville's day, the walls were covered in ivy and the green shutters were used to screen the rooms from damaging sunlight.

THE WEST FRONT

Unlike the east and south fronts, this remains exactly as designed by Poynter in 1903–5, with its central pediment and pierced balustrade alluding to the similar, if not identical, elements of the entrance façade. To the right is a Palladian stone screen fronting the small loggia, and, to the left, facing south, is a pergola supported by Ionic columns on Elizabethan-style bases. On this side, apart from the windows above the loggia, there are no painted shutters, and light-protection for the rooms within was originally provided by external blinds.

THE CENTRAL COURTYARD

This Italianate lawned court remains as designed by Poynter in 1903–5, except that his central fountain has long disappeared. In 1996 the limestone well-head was moved from the north-west side of the house to its present position. The well-head was originally a column capital, and although most elements of its decoration can be paralleled in 12th-century Byzantine sculpture, it seems to have been made in Italy, probably in Venice. The set of terracotta pots is probably Italian, late 19th-century.

POLESDEN LACEY

Surrey

THE NATIONAL TRUST

Acknowledgements

For help with this guidebook, I am particularly grateful to Sir Nicholas Bonsor, Bt, Mrs Ann Davis-Thomas, Mr David H. Smith and Mrs Alma Topen, who have allowed access to original material and who have shared their knowledge of Polesden and its family connections. For research assistance, I owe much to Tracey Avery, Sophie Chessum, Brian Godfrey, Martin Higgins, Charles O'Brien, Nino Strachey and Colin White. The descriptions of the maiolica derive from J. V. G. Mallet's 1971 catalogue (and his unpublished revisions); those of the porcelain and silver from lists compiled by Anthony du Boulay and the late M. D. G. Clayton. The picture entries are based on St John Gore's catalogue (1964, revised 1971), on notes by Alastair Laing (who has also helped in other ways) and on the relevant section of Richard Walker's forthcoming catalogue of the Trust's miniatures. Details on the tapestries were provided by the Franses Research Archive. The chapter on the garden, park and estate draws on unpublished reports by Christopher Currie and Katie Fretwell. I am also indebted to numerous individuals and institutions for help and scholarly information, including Madelaine Abey-Koch, Agnew's, Mary Rose Blacker, John Bonsor, Christie's, Colnaghi's, English Heritage, Harry Fane, Sallyann Hardwick, John Hart, Georgia Hedley, Simon Jervis, the Rev. Leslie Jollie, Linda Kelly, John Kenworthy-Browne, Tim Knox, Julia Lloyd-Williams, Robert Morris, the National Monuments Record, Lord Plunket, Eileen Reay, the Royal Collections Trust, the Royal Scottish Academy and Delia Webster. At Polesden, Paul Dearn was a constant source of support. Oliver Garnett edited the book and suggested many improvements.

Christopher Rowell

Photographs: Country Life Picture Library p. 58; Illustrated London News Picture Library pp. 40, 74; A. F. Kersting p. 50; National Trust pp. 44, 45, 48, 49, 52, 53, 57, 70, 76; National Trust Photographic Library p. 75; NTPL/John Bethell pp. 34, 63, 65; NTPL/Andreas von Einsiedel front cover, pp. 1, 3, 4, 8, 9, 10, 11, 13, 16, 26, 27, 29, 30, 31, 33, 35, 37, 60, 67, 68, 69, 71, 79, back cover; NTPL/John Hammond pp. 23, 25, 55; NTPL/Angelo Hornak p. 15; NTPL/Nadia Mackenzie p. 59; NTPL/Nick Meers pp. 7, 42, 47, 77; NTPL/Derrick E. Witty pp. 14, 18, 19, 20, 21, 38, 56, 62, 64, 66, 72; private collection p. 51; Westminster City Archives p. 73.

ISBN 1-84359-040-9

Designed by James Shurmer

Phototypeset in Monotype Bembo Series 270
by Intraspan Ltd, Smallfield, Surrey (SG1460)

Print managed by Astron
for the National Trust (Enterprises) Ltd,
Heelis, Kemble Drive, Swindon, Wiltshire SN2 2NA

(*Front cover*) The western arm of the Picture Corridor is dominated by Carolus-Duran's portrait of Mrs Greville

(*Title-page*) Mrs Greville's love of dogs encouraged her to buy these Fabergé creatures in the Saloon

(*Back cover*) The Saloon

(*Opposite*) Detail of the south Italian gilt panelling, *c.*1700, in the Saloon

CONTENTS

The east front

The Interior

THE ENTRANCE HALL

This porch was constructed to Poynter's design in 1903–5, together, presumably, with the glazed screen looking through to the Central Hall.

FURNISHINGS

The 1943 inventory and an undated list of fittings and curtains are the principal sources for the furnishing of the house in Mrs Greville's time. The Entrance Hall still contains much of its original late Victorian and Edwardian furniture: the 'two oak umbrella stands with brass bands', the 'oak pedestal letter box' and the mahogany barometer. The 'four pairs of crimson cut velvet curtains' still survive in store, but are now beyond repair and have been replaced by copies.

SCULPTURE

JOHN HUTCHISON, RSA (1833–1910)
Five signed and dated marble portrait busts: (no. 1) of William McEwan, father of Mrs Greville, dated Edinburgh, 1885 (the year of his marriage to Mrs Greville's mother), and four unidentified female subjects. The bust of a girl (no. 3, Edinburgh, 1870), to the right of the Central Hall door, has a socle matching that of McEwan's bust, so his must have been placed next to it, albeit fifteen years later. The bust of a young girl (no. 4, Edinburgh, 1880), on the left-hand window-sill, is traditionally believed to be of Mrs Greville (b. 1863), an impossibility given that she was then seventeen. These busts may in fact be idealised genre heads of Roman girls, which were Hutchison's speciality.

The 13th-century columnar holy water stoup supported by a recumbent lion was made in Lombardy, north Italy, of Veronese marble. It was presumably acquired by Mrs Greville, perhaps through her decorators, White, Allom & Co.

THE CENTRAL HALL

Apart from the fireplace wall with its magnificent late 17th-century carved woodwork, the Central Hall remains as designed by Poynter in 1903–5, with oak work by Messrs White of Bedford and carving by Lawrence Turner. Like Poynter's other Polesden interiors, the original effect was rather Spartan, enlivened only by the odd trophy of arms.

In c.1906–9 Mrs Greville's decorators, White,

7

Allom & Co., installed the reredos around the fireplace, and possibly were also responsible for bringing in at least some of the furniture and tapestries depicted in a photograph of 1921 and described in the 1943 inventory.

In Mrs Greville's day, the Central Hall was not only intended for the reception and departure of guests (the cloakroom, wardrobes and lavatory were adjoining), but was also used as a sitting-room, where 'every evening at six o'clock, the footman used to lay out the drinks', according to the writer Beverley Nichols.

CARVINGS

FIREPLACE WALL:

The oak panelling and decorative carvings (now with certain modifications and omissions) originally formed the reredos of St Matthew's, Friday Street, the cheapest and plainest of all Sir Christopher Wren's City churches, which was rebuilt after the Great Fire of 1666 in 1682–5. Wren's mason in charge of the work was Edward Pierce (*c.*1630–95), an architect, craftsman and collector who is best known as a sculptor and carver in the style now primarily associated with Grinling Gibbons. Pierce carved all the woodwork for St Matthew's, including this altarpiece, in collaboration with the joiner Richard Kedge. Edward Hatton's *New View of London* (1708) gives a precise description of the altarpiece *in situ*:

[It] is adorned with 2 fluted Columns, and Entablature, and Compass-pediment, of the *Corinthian* order; [in] the Intercolumniations are the Commandments in gilt frames, and done in gold Letters on Black under a Cherubim; without [ie outside] the Columns, are the Lord's Prayer and Creed done in Black on Gold, each under a small triangular pediment [the inscriptions have been replaced by the pair of double doors], where is placed on two shields J. R. [ie Johannes Rex for James II] and the Queen's Arms ... and the whole Altar-piece has Enrichments of 4 Lamps [two survive]; also Festoons, Fruit, Leaves, &c, all of oak.

In 1766 the decoration was altered slightly, and then radically in 1862, when much more gilding was applied. In 1883 the church was demolished, and its furnishings were put up for auction. The reredos was later acquired by White, Allom & Co., who suggested installing it here. Victorian drawings show that much of the original carving has been lost (for example, within the central pediment) and that the reredos was altered to fit into its present

The carving by Edward Pierce around the Central Hall fireplace came originally from St Matthew's, Friday Street, one of Christopher Wren's City churches, built in 1682–5

position. It was reduced in height (approximately 20 cm was removed from the plinths of the columns), widened at the sides to accommodate the double doors, the centre was broken forward around the chimneybreast, and a new marble chimneypiece in 17th-century style replaced the altar table (and Poynter's wooden fire-surround).

CHANDELIER

The massive silver-plated late Victorian chandelier in 17th-century French style was introduced after Mrs Greville's remodelling of the room and may have been supplied by White, Allom & Co., as presumably were the similar silver-plated sconces.

FURNITURE

The oak table with carved frieze is English, early 17th-century (with restorations).

A set of walnut seat furniture comprising a sofa and six armchairs is provincial French, *c.*1735. The *gros point* tapestry upholstery is probably 19th-century.

The lacquered and gilt octagonal tripod table is *c.*1860; its glazed top is mounted with a panel of French needlework, *c.*1750. Listed here in 1943.

CARPETS

ON CENTRAL TABLE:

The rug is Persian (Kirman), second half of the 19th century.

IN FRONT OF FIREPLACE:

The rug is Persian (Bidjar), in a Herati design, first half of the 20th century.

PORCELAIN

ON RADIATOR COVERS:

The pair of blue-and-white covered jars is Chinese, Kangxi (1662–1722).

TAPESTRIES

FIREPLACE WALL, CENTRE:

Attributed to LEO VAN DEN HECKE
? *An Episode from the Life of Caesar and Cleopatra*
From a set of eight, and definitely made in Brussels in the 16th century, the subject is unclear and may also represent a scene in the life of Alexander the Great.

EITHER SIDE:

FLEMISH, *c*.1700
Dido and Aeneas
Two tapestries from a group of three (the other, larger, tapestry is hanging opposite) and originally from a larger set.

WALL OPPOSITE FIREPLACE, CENTRE:

FLEMISH, *c*.1700
A Scene from the Story of Aeneas

EITHER SIDE:

BRUSSELS, second half of the 17th century
The Kermesse, or Village Fête
The figures and style of the tapestries (originally elements of a single tapestry) were inspired by the paintings of David Teniers the Younger (1610–90), court painter and curator to the Archduke Leopold Wilhelm, Habsburg governor of the Spanish Netherlands.

THE STAIRCASE LANDING

PICTURE

123 Attributed to GIOVANNI BATTISTA VIOLA
(1576–1622)
River Landscape with Figures
Viola was an early specialist in landscape, a pupil of Annibale Carracci, and a collaborator and imitator of Albani and Domenichino (to whom this picture is closest in style). Possibly also by Viola's pupil, Pietro Paolo Bonzi.

FURNITURE

The mahogany longcase clock is by Robert Mawley, London, *c*.1750. Its chiming dial offers a choice of eight bells or 'As St Mary's Cambridge'.

MAIOLICA

From the 15th century, Hispano-Moresque wares were imported into Italy via Majorca, and Italian imitations of this tin-glazed earthenware became known as 'maiolica'. Maiolica was decorated with both pictorial compositions and abstract designs, and, in its most elaborate form, was designed both for use at banquets and for display on sideboards.

16 *Dish on low foot*, Urbino, with lustre pigments added at Gubbio, *c*.1535–40, by a painter close to Francesco Xanto Avelli. Taken from an engraving

A maiolica plate, made in Deruta c.1520 (Staircase Landing)

after Raphael, the painting depicts the rape of Lucretia, a married Roman woman, who according to legend committed suicide after being raped by Sextus, son of the tyrant Tarquin the Proud.

17 *Dish on low foot*, Urbino, *c*.1528–30, painted by Francesco Xanto Avelli, with a figure of Charity copied from an engraving by Marcantonio Raimondi (*c*.1475–*c*.1534) after Raphael.

18 *Plate*, Urbino, *c*.1527–30, painted by Francesco Xanto Avelli with an *Allegory of the Sack of Rome in 1527*. The figure of the Tiber holds a cornucopia symbolising the riches of the Holy City and rests his right hand on a sphere, which is probably a ball or *pallone*, an emblem of the Medici family. Clement VII (de' Medici) was Pope at the time of the capture of Rome by troops of the Holy Roman Emperor, Charles V.

19a, b *Two plates with deep centres (tondini)*, painted with a scale-like pattern in yellow lustre and blue, Deruta, *c*.1520.

20 *Plate with deep centre*, painted in blue monochrome with, in the centre, a turbaned head, Deruta, *c*.1524.

21 *Plate* with a bust of a woman in profile in the centre and a scale pattern border, Deruta, *c*.1500–10.

22 *Plate*, School of Urbino, attributed to Francesco Durantino, dated 1544 on reverse. It depicts the Greek hero Perseus's rescue of Andromeda, the daughter of an Ethiopian king, who was chained to a rock as a sacrifice to a sea-monster (Ovid, *Metamorphoses*, 5, 665–739). Bought for £84 at the Cook sale in 1925 by Tancred Borenius, presumably on Mrs Greville's behalf.

23 *Plate painted with the Finding of Moses*, Urbino, *c.*1540–6.

24 *Dish on low foot*, Castel Durante; *c.*1524–6, attributed to the so-called 'In Castel Durante Painter'. The subject (*The Judgement of Paris*) is loosely derived from a famous engraving after Raphael by Marcantonio Raimondi. Bought for £315 at the Cook sale in 1925 by Borenius.

25 *Plate*, Urbino, *c.*1530, painted by Francesco Xanto Avelli and depicting Cupid, Psyche and a River God, with an unidentified coat of arms. Cupid's love for Psyche eventually led to their marriage and guaranteed her immortality, according to a late 2nd-century AD fairy tale by Lucino Apulcino. From the Harris collection.

26 *Plate*, Urbino, 1532, signed and dated on the reverse by Francesco Xanto Avelli, with a scene from Ovid's *Metamorphoses* (11, 1–43): *The Thracian Maenads turned into trees for the murder of Orpheus* (the legendary poet and musician, husband of Eurydice). From a large service bearing the arms of Pucci beneath a Papal *ombrellino*, this dish was formerly in the Bernal and Harris collections.

27 *Dish on low foot*, Urbino, *c.*1535–40. It originally formed part of a service made for Giacomo Nordi, Bishop of Urbino 1523–40, and bears his coat of arms. The subject (*Aesculapius restoring Hippolytus to life*) is taken from Ovid's *Metamorphoses*. From the Harris collection.

28 *Plate*, Urbino, dated 1534 on the reverse, studio of Francesco Xanto Avelli, who may have painted the three adult heads. According to legend, Leander, the lover of Hero, a priestess of Aphrodite, was drowned while swimming the Hellespont to visit her. Hero, in despair, threw herself into the sea. From the Harris collection.

29 *Figure of a duck*, Urbino, *c.*1573; perhaps from the workshop of Flaminio Fontana, who supplied Cardinal Ferdinando de' Medici with three ducks as part of a large delivery of maiolica in 1573.

30, 31, 32 *Three figures of parrots or hawks*, Urbino, *c.*1570–5. These rare models of birds (possibly from the Palazzo Albani, Rome) were bought at the Cook sale in 1925 for £110 5s by Borenius.

33 *Plate with deep centre*, with, in the centre, a polychrome profile bust and the inscription 'LUCIO', Faenza, *c.*1525. Bought by Borenius in 1925 for £89 5s from the Cook collection.

34 *Plate*, Faenza, decorated in the centre with a young woman singing, the border with scroll-ornament and dated 1537.

35 *Plate*, Urbino, dated 1534 on the reverse, probably by a painter close to Francesco Xanto Avelli, depicting the story of Pyramus and Thisbe, the figures being derived from engravings. Ovid (*Metamorphoses*, 4, 55–166) tells how Pyramus, thinking his lover has been killed by a lion, stabs himself with a sword. On discovering his corpse, Thisbe falls on his sword. From the Harris collection.

45 *Ewer (for wine or water)*, perhaps French (?Nevers), *c.*1600. The biblical subject (the sons of Jacob answering Schechem and Hamor; *Genesis* 34) is copied from an engraving by Bernard Salomon (1506/10–*c.*1561). From the Spitzer collection.

248 *Small plate*, Urbino, *c.*1540–5, in the style of Francesco Durantino, one of the most productive maiolica painters, who presumably originated from

Italian maiolica parrots or hawks, made in Urbino, c.1570–75 (Staircase Landing)

Castel Durante. The Old Testament Apocrypha records how Susanna, the wife of a prosperous Jew living in Babylon, resisted two Elders' attempt to rape her in her bath. Bought for £52 10s in 1925 at the Cook sale by Borenius.

256 *Dish* painted with a female head and a scroll inscribed 'Flaminia Bella', probably Castel Durante, *c*.1530. This was the most expensive (£483) of Borenius's purchases, as Mrs Greville's agent, at the sale in 1925 of the Cook collection of maiolica.

THE BLUE CLOAK ROOM

This little room off the Central Hall to the left was the 'Blue Cloak Room' in Mrs Greville's day, where guests left their coats. Beyond is a wardrobe room and lavatory (not open at present).

PAST FURNISHINGS

In 1943 the curtains were of blue striped silk, the carpet of blue felt with two Persian rugs in complementary colours. The chairs were 'Windsor armchairs, with interlaced arch-shaped backs' (part of the Picture Corridor set), there was a mirror for checking one's appearance, and several carriage rugs of sable and lynx fur lined with blue cloth. The room was hung with numerous engravings including 65 Parisian costume prints, some of which survived the 1943 sales.

PRESENT FURNISHINGS

Of the room's 1943 contents, still *in situ* are the Victorian giltwood overmantel mirror and the overdoor garniture of 'Three Delft vases and covers' (late 18th-century). The room is now hung with three designs and one ground plan (1907) for new formal gardens drawn up by Durand, Murray & Seddon, but never executed. There is also a map of Polesden (1818) by A. and E. Driver.

THE DINING ROOM

This room, with its elliptical ends and niche in the west wall, remains as designed by Poynter in 1903–5. To the right of the fireplace is a jib door leading to the Serving Room, Kitchen and other offices (not open). The late 18th-century white marble chimneypiece was probably introduced by

Mrs Greville, who certainly hung the room with pink silk damask (the present hangings are replacements, in a different pattern, made after the fire of 1960).

PAST FURNISHINGS

Most of the furniture listed in 1943 was sold the same year. The dining-table was described as a 'lacquer circular table, decorated with foliage in black and gold, the top mounted with panels of point de Venice [*sic*] lace beneath glass'. This American style of table, first mentioned in 1934, replaced a traditional English dining-table, which was always covered with a linen tablecloth (as at Charles Street, where the same change was made). Previously, Mrs Greville had been known for her conservatism in arranging her table, resisting modern innovations such as table mats, and remaining loyal to Edwardian conventions. The display of old silver was particularly remarked upon, and by 1933 such was the profusion of silver that it had entirely taken 'the place of flowers on Mrs Greville's table'. There were 22 mahogany dining-chairs: twelve 'of Hepplewhite design, with shield-shaped backs' upholstered in pink damask (presumably matching the damask of curtains and walls) and ten with 'backs carved with drapery festoons' and 'pink and silver silk' upholstery. The remaining furniture included two marble-topped giltwood side-tables 'with winged caryatid figures on the legs', a serving-table, plate-carrier, two dumb-waiters, two four-leaf screens and other practical late 19th- or early 20th-century pieces, which were considered unworthy of preservation and were sold by the Trust in 1943. Apart from the dining-table, there was no other lacquer furniture in the Dining Room in Mrs Greville's day.

PICTURES

The present arrangement, predominantly of British portraits, is the Trust's post-war re-hang, but probably reflects how the room appeared in its heyday. Beverley Nichols remembered Winston Churchill at Polesden, holding forth about the German menace 'with a good cigar in one hand and a better Armagnac in the other' during his 'finest hour' after dinner [in 1930] with 'behind him … one of Raeburn's finest pictures, The Paterson Children' (no. 7). It was normal late Victorian and Edwardian practice to congregate such supremely fashionable

The Dining Room

and expensive British portraits in single rooms (as Sir Julius Wernher did at Bath House, Piccadilly).

RIGHT OF ENTRANCE DOOR:

2 JONATHAN RICHARDSON the Elder (1665–1745)
Self-portrait
One of the first pictures bought by Mrs Greville (in 1916 for £200), it has probably hung here ever since (listed in the Dining Room in 1943). Richardson (a prolific self-portraitist) combined portraiture with poetry, literature, criticism and writings on art: eg *An Essay on the Theory of Painting* (1715) and *An Account of Some of the Statues [etc.] in Italy* (1722). He was also a notable collector of drawings.

WALL OPPOSITE WINDOWS:

5 JACOB HUYSMANS (*c.*1633–96)
An Unknown Woman
Huysmans arrived in England from Antwerp in 1662 and was particularly favoured by the Queen,

Catherine of Braganza, and her Catholic courtiers. Bought by William McEwan in 1900.

4 BENJAMIN CONSTANT (1845–1902)
William McEwan (1827–1913), 1900
Mrs Greville's beloved father was a self-made millionaire brewer, whose native Scotland was the focus for his considerable philanthropy. He bought Polesden Lacey for his only daughter and son-in-law in 1906 and paid for its remodelling. On his death, Mrs Greville inherited his fortune, his collection of pictures and his town house, 16 Charles Street, Mayfair.

According to Mrs Greville, 'my Father disliked [this] picture. B. C. [Benjamin Constant] loved it ... [and] considered it his chef d'oeuvre'. This 'striking likeness' was painted 'hurriedly' in six sittings at the Savoy Hotel at a cost of £1,200. It has always hung here. Constant specialised in Orientalist pictures in the 1870s and 1880s, later concentrating on portraits and large decorative projects.

3 Studio of Sir PETER LELY (1618–80)
*Lady Elizabeth Wriothesley, Countess of
Northumberland* (d. 1690)
Daughter of the 4th and last Earl of Southampton,
and thus a great heiress. She married the 11th and
last Earl of Northumberland (1644–70) in 1662, and
in 1673 Ralph Montagu (later 1st Earl and Duke of
Montagu).

FIREPLACE WALL:

6 Sir HENRY RAEBURN, RA (1756–1823)
Isabella Simpson
The wife of William Simpson (d. 1808), a director
of the Royal Bank of Scotland, whose portrait by
Raeburn (pendant to no. 6) is still in the possession
of his descendants. Purchased for £2,500 in 1896 by
McEwan from his principal supplier of Dutch Old
Masters, the London dealer Lesser Adrian Lesser.

OVER CHIMNEYPIECE:

9 Sir JOSHUA REYNOLDS, PRA (1723–92)
Nymph and Piping Boy
Inspired by Titian, the painting has suffered from
Reynolds's use of bitumen. But such was the fashion

*Isabella Simpson; by Sir Henry Raeburn (no. 6; Dining
Room)*

for these 'fancy' pictures that Mrs Greville paid
Agnew's the huge sum of £7,410 for it in 1917,
despite its condition.

8 Sir HENRY RAEBURN, RA (1756–1823)
George and Maria Stewart as Children
The children of Dugald Stewart (1753–1828),
Professor of Moral Philosophy at Edinburgh, and
Helen Cranstoun, whom he married in 1790.
Bought for £5,500 by Mrs Greville from Colnaghi's
in 1919.

WALL OPPOSITE FIREPLACE:

11 Sir THOMAS LAWRENCE, PRA (1769–1830)
The Masters Pattisson
William (1801–32) and Jacob (1803–74) were the
sons of W.H. Pattisson of Witham, Essex, for
whom Lawrence painted the picture in 1811–17.
William and his wife were to drown on their
honeymoon. Lawrence had considerable difficulty
finishing the portrait, which the family sold in 1860
for 200 guineas. Mrs Greville paid Agnew's
£12,000 in 1918.

10 Sir HENRY RAEBURN, RA (1756–1823)
Sir William Macleod Bannatyne (1743–1833)
A Scottish judge whose literary interests were
evident in his contributions to Edinburgh period-
icals. He 'was among the last of the Scotch gentlemen ... who could make use of the graphic and
strong vernacular Scotch in the pure and beautiful
form in which, for many years after the union, it
continued to be the current speech of the Scotch
upper classes.' Bought by McEwan for £367 10s in
1897.

7 Sir HENRY RAEBURN, RA (1756–1823)
The Paterson Children
Painted *c*.1790; the children are George (1778–
1846), later Colonel of the 3rd Foot Guards; John
(1778–1858), a naval captain; and Margaret (d. 1845),
whose parents, George and Anne Paterson, of
Castle Huntly, Perthshire, were also painted by
Raeburn. Sold by the family to Agnew's in 1913
and acquired by Mrs Greville in 1918 for £23,000,
by far the highest price she ever paid for a picture.

FURNITURE

RIGHT OF ENTRANCE DOOR:

The small lacquer bureau on stand is Chinese, 18th-
century; the stand is English.

WALL OPPOSITE WINDOWS:

The lacquer chest is English, late 19th-century, with japanned chinoiserie decoration in 18th-century style.

The bombé commode, incorporating panels of Chinese lacquer bordered with English japanning and mounted in ormolu, is English, *c.*1760–5, in the style associated with Pierre Langlois (active 1759–81), a Parisian *ébéniste* who was practising in London by 1759. Commodes of this quality were never meant to be used.

FIREPLACE WALL:

The mahogany chairs with lattice backs (two groups of three from larger sets) in the Chinese Chippendale style are probably 19th-century.

WALL OPPOSITE FIREPLACE:

The secrétaire à abattant (upright desk with fall-front), veneered with black and gold Chinese lacquer and mounted in ormolu, was made in 1745. It is stamped eight times by its maker, the *ébéniste* and dealer Jean-Baptiste Tuart *père* (*c.*1700–*c.*1767; *maître* 1741), and also by its retailer, Léonard Boudin (1735–1807; *maître* 1761).

The pair of Boulle glazed cabinets is French, *c.*1790, in the style of Louis XIV's principal *ébéniste*, André-Charles Boulle (1642–1732), who gave his name to this type of metal-inlaid wood and tortoiseshell furniture. The cabinets are on loan from the Phillimore family and, by tradition, were made for Stowe, Buckinghamshire.

CENTRE OF ROOM:

The mahogany dining-table is English, *c.*1800. It is not original to the room (see above) and, indeed, may not be indigenous to Polesden Lacey.

The eight mahogany dining-chairs are late 19th-century in the style of Thomas Chippendale.

WALL LIGHTS

The set of giltwood two-branched sconces was listed in 1943 as of 'Adam design' and was presumably made around 1900.

SCULPTURE

ON MANTELPIECE, CENTRE:

The bronze bust (on a later white marble plinth), of the Emperor Vitellius (reigned AD 69), is Italian, late 16th-century.

The Paterson Children; by Sir Henry Raeburn, c.1790 (no. 7; Dining Room). Mrs Greville's most expensive picture

CENTRE LEFT:

The bronze statuette of the Piping Faun is Italian, probably 18th-century, after a much-copied Antique Roman statue (Paris, Louvre), which is itself a copy of a lost Greek bronze of the second half of the 4th century BC.

CENTRE RIGHT:

The bronze statuette of Amphitrite, wife of Neptune, is after a model made in 1652 by Michel Anguier (1612/14–86), a French sculptor who had worked in Rome *c.*1641–51.

FAR LEFT AND RIGHT:

The two bronze horses are 17th-century, after models by Francesco Fanelli (active *c.*1609–*c.*1665), a Florentine sculptor who came to England in the early 1630s and worked for Charles I and his court.

CLOCK

The ormolu wall-clock with enamel dial in Rococo style, is French, *c.*1760–5. The movement is modern. Here in 1943.

SILVER

ON DINING-TABLE (LOOKING TOWARDS FIREPLACE):

The three circular salvers on trumpet feet (bearing fruit) are: (left) maker's mark ?TR, London, 1692; (centre) maker's mark TS, London, 1683; and (right) probably by Robert Peake, London, 1706.

The four tankards (on either side of the central salver) are (left) maker's mark WC, London, 1674; (far left) maker's mark IS [?John Sutton], London, 1678, with later chinoiserie engraving; (right) maker's mark RN, London, 1691; and (far right) maker's mark TL, London, 1674.

The pair of single candlesticks is by John Horsley, London, 1762.

The two porringers and covers with chinoiserie engraving (at either end of the table) are (left) maker's mark FS, London, 1683 (engraving original); and (right) maker's mark FW, London, 1689 (engraving modern).

The sugar casters are English, early 18th-century, and include the remnants of two slightly larger matched groups of casters (three were sold in 1943) by Anthony Nelme (a pair, 1721) and Charles Adams (1709, 1714 and 1716).

IN BOULLE GLAZED CABINETS:

LEFT-HAND CABINET, TOP SHELF:

Robert Timbrell, London, 1699 (with later chinoiserie engraving); David Williams, London, 1701.

MIDDLE SHELF:

A pair of mugs with chinoiserie engraving, London, 1685, and *a tankard*, London, 1713, by George and Francis Garthorne, respectively.

BOTTOM SHELF:

A mug, marked IG, London, dated 1682, 1694 or 1696; *a salver on trumpet foot* by Thomas Bolton, Dublin, 1693–5; *a tankard* marked FS, London, 1690.

RIGHT-HAND CABINET, TOP SHELF:

Porringer by Robert Timbrell, London, 1704 (with later armorials); *mug*, marked EG, London, 1692; *porringer*, marked Pe (?Edward Peacock), London, 1711 (with later armorials).

(Opposite) The south arm of the Picture Corridor

MIDDLE SHELF:

Three porringers: London, 1689; marked GS, London, 1680 (chasing and finial probably not original); London, 1685.

BOTTOM SHELF:

Porringer, marked FS, London, 1683 (later armorials); *mug*, marked R or TR, London, 1689; and *porringer*, marked TI, London, 1685.

PORCELAIN

ON DINING-TABLE:

The dessert plates (from a larger set) are continental, in the style of the Zurich factory, late 19th-century.

ON SIDEBOARD:

The tureen is continental, late 19th-century.

THE PICTURE CORRIDOR

The Picture Corridor runs around three sides of the central quadrangle and was adapted from the previously existing corridor by Poynter *c.*1903–5. Mrs Greville inserted the barrel vault and oak panelling in 1906–9. Her work was carried out under the direction of Arthur Davis (for Mewès and Davis), probably by White, Allom & Co., who specialised in architectural salvage (the panelling is Jacobean cut to fit), with Jackson's, the London plasterers who made the ceiling (copied from the Long Gallery of 1607–12 at Chastleton, Oxfordshire).

FURNISHINGS

White, Allom & Co. probably also supplied the antiquarian set of ten 'iron hall lanterns', which were supplemented by brass picture lights (improved copies were installed in 1997). Natural light was regulated, as today, by full-length shutters on the courtyard windows. The red chenille carpet (*c.*1906–9) was originally complemented by matching red silk curtains with darker red cut-silk velvet damask curtains at either end of the main section of the Picture Corridor. These curtains, their tie-backs and sun curtains, which were removed by the Trust soon after the war, are now being gradually replaced as funds permit. (An original pair of the cut-silk velvet curtains hangs at the west end of the south arm of the Picture Corridor and both the original appliqué silk velvet pelmets also survive.)

The Antique Roman sarcophagus has recently been returned to the centre of the principal arm of the Corridor flanked by two north Italian marquetry chests-of-drawers, as shown in two early photographs, and other changes have been made to reflect the room's appearance in 1943: the grouping together of the 16th- and early 17th-century French and Flemish furniture at the south-west corner of the Picture Corridor; the mixture of continental furniture upholstered in *gros point* tapestry or damask; the showcases, porcelain jars and the oak Windsor chairs. The 1943 inventory also lists an '"HMV" Radio-Gramaphone, in walnut case', which in a 1926 photograph is shown placed strategically for the Central Hall, where dancing sometimes took place.

PICTURES

Although the Picture Corridor was intended principally to display paintings, during Mrs Greville's life most of her best pictures were hung at Charles Street.

(In numerical order rather than by location; no. 1 is on an easel at the far end of the western arm of the Picture Corridor)

1 CHARLES-AUGUSTE-EMILE DURAND, known as CAROLUS-DURAN (1837–1917)
Margaret Anderson, the Hon. Mrs Ronald Greville, DBE (1863–1942), 1891
Painted in the year of her marriage to the Hon. Ronald Greville (1864–1908), this bravura portrait shows ample evidence of Carolus-Duran's technical accomplishment. He taught his students (Sargent among them) to paint *au premier coup* (stroke by stroke without reworking).

Mrs Greville was the natural daughter of the Scottish millionaire brewer and philanthropist William McEwan, whose fortune enabled her to maintain her position as one of the supreme hostesses of her generation. She was noted for her caustic wit, as a collector both of royalties and works of art, and, more notoriously, for her pro-Nazi sympathies in the 1930s. She bequeathed Polesden Lacey and most of her other property to the National Trust in 1942, in memory of her father – one of the first such benefactions of a country house and its collections.

(Right) An Unknown Woman; by Corneille de Lyon, c.1535–40 (no. 14; Picture Corridor)

12 After QUINTEN MASSYS (1465/6–1530)
An Unknown Man
Acquired by Mrs Greville soon after 1934; companion to no. 13. Massys was the leading painter of early 16th-century Antwerp. Faithful, and apparently early, copies of two pictures in the Altrincham collection.

13 After QUINTEN MASSYS (1465/6–1530)
An Unknown Woman
Companion to no. 12.

14 CORNEILLE DE LYON (active 1533–74)
An Unknown Woman
Corneille de Lyon was painter to the Dauphin from 1541, and *peintre du roi* from 1548, when he became Henri II. Sold with a small group of masterpieces from Petworth in 1927 and acquired the same year from Agnew's by Mrs Greville. Datable from the costume to *c.*1535–40.

15 CORNEILLE DE LYON (active 1533–74)
An Unknown Man, called James V of Scotland (1512–42)
Formally inscribed on the back '*Le Roi agé 25*', but more probably of a Lyons courtier called Le Roi than of the King. Bought at Sotheby's in 1922 by Tancred Borenius acting as Mrs Greville's agent.

16 Style of CORNEILLE DE LYON (active 1533–74)
An Unknown Man wearing ermine
The ermine denotes a nobleman.

17 CORNEILLE DE LYON (active 1533–74)
Catherine de' Medici (1519–89)
Wife of Henri II of France, whose initial 'H' she
wears as a jewel. No doubt painted when the Queen
visited the painter's studio in Lyons in 1536. From
the collection of Louis XIV's minister for the arts,
Colbert.

*(Nos. 18–22 hang at the south-west [far] end of the main
corridor)*

18 FRANCESCUCCIO GHISSI (active 1359–74)
The Madonna of Humility and other scenes
Ghissi was the main follower in the Marches of
Allegretto Nuzi (1316/20–1373/4), whose works
inspired him. The central panel depicts the Madonna
of Humility, a type that originated in Siena and
became popular after the Black Death in 1348. The
Virgin is portrayed seated humbly on the ground,
humility being regarded in medieval theology as
the root of all other virtues. The wings of the triptych depict (left) the *Nativity* and (right) the
Crucifixion, with the *Annunciation* in the gabled
tops.

19 Workshop of BARTOLO DI FREDI
(*c.*1330–1410)
The Adoration of the Magi
A Sienese painter also active in San Gimignano,
Montalcino and Volterra, who also occupied
several municipal posts in Siena. This is a simplified
variant of a painting in the Pinacoteca in Siena
(no. 104).

20 Attributed to PIETRO PERUGINO
(*c.*1450–1523)
The Miracle of the Founding of Santa Maria Maggiore
Part of a predella to a lost altarpiece, probably
painted in Florence *c.*1475, it depicts the miraculous
fall of snow on 5 August 352, which traced the plan
of Santa Maria Maggiore, Rome, as foretold in a
vision of the Virgin Mary to Pope Liberius. Perugino was later Raphael's teacher and takes his name
from his birthplace, Perugia in central Italy. Bought
as a Filippino Lippi by Mrs Greville through Dr
Borenius from Charles Langton Douglas, another
prominent scholar-dealer (see p.65), and hung in
her boudoir at Polesden.

*The Adoration of the Magi; workshop of Bartolo di Fredi
(no. 19; Picture Corridor)*

21 BYZANTINE, possibly VENETIAN, first half of
14th century
The Virgin and Child enthroned with Saints
The gabled tops of this portable altarpiece contain
depictions of the *Annunciation* (at either side) and of
the *Crucifixion* (centre). The saints shown (particularly SS Francis and Dominic) indicate that it was
painted in Italy. The representation of St Louis of
Toulouse (d. 1297) suggests a date after his canonisa-
tion in 1317.

22 LUCA DI TOMMÈ (active 1356–89)
*The Madonna and Child with St John the Baptist and
(?) St Catherine*
The central panel of a triptych by this Sienese artist,
who was principally influenced by the Lorenzetti
brothers. Probably an early work, painted before
1362.

23 MASTER OF ST SEVERIN (active *c.*1485–*c.*1515)
An Old Woman
The artist derives his name from two panels (*c.*1500)
in the church of St Severin, Cologne, and was one

A River Scene with a Ferryboat; by Salomon van Ruysdael, 1647 (no. 31; Picture Corridor)

of the first portrait-painters of the Cologne school. This example, of *c.*1500, has an unusual and well-preserved red ground. It belonged to the pioneering Cologne collector of 'Primitives', Bernard Lyversberg (1761–1833), many of whose finest treasures are now in the Wallraf-Richartz Museum in Cologne.

24 BAREND VAN ORLEY (active *c.*1488–d. 1541)
The Madonna and Child
Orley worked in Brussels, but was much influenced by Raphael. He also produced designs for tapestries and stained glass, such as that in the Chapel at The Vyne, Hampshire.

25 JACOB LEVECQ (1634–75)
A Young Man
Apparently once bore the signature of Levecq, the date 1654, and the unknown sitter's age: 19. The earliest known work by this Dordrecht-based pupil of Rembrandt.

26 BENEDETTO DIANA (RUSCONI) (*c.*1460–1525)
The Meeting of Joachim and Anne
According to the *Golden Legend*, Joachim, a rich man, and Anne, his wife (barren after twenty years of marriage), were separately instructed by an angel to meet at the Golden Gate at Jerusalem. At the appointed place, they embraced joyfully and from that moment Anne was pregnant with Mary, the mother of Jesus. A fragment of a predella by a follower of Giovanni Bellini, acquired by Mrs Greville and originally hung in her boudoir.

30 AERT VAN DER NEER (1603/4–77)
A Town on a Frozen River
This Amsterdam artist specialised in winter and night scenes, being particularly interested in dramatic effects of light and shade. Painted *c.*1645–50. Bought by McEwan for £756 in 1893 from the Mildmay collection via Lesser.

31 SALOMON VAN RUYSDAEL (1600/3–70)
A River Scene with a Ferryboat, 1647
The uncle of Jacob van Ruisdael (see no. 53), this Haarlem painter often employed the horizontal motif of a crowded ferryboat. Bought by McEwan

in 1893 from the Mildmay collection via Lesser for £913 10s.

32 ?ISAACK VAN OSTADE (1621–49)
A Village Inn
A native of Haarlem, where he was taught by his brother, Adriaen (see no. 49). Isaack painted mostly outdoor rustic scenes, on a large scale, and with greater boldness. Bought from Lesser by McEwan for £1,575 in 1893. Certain weaknesses may indicate the hand of an imitator.

33 WILLEM VAN DE VELDE the Younger
(1633–1707) or ? Studio
Shipping in a Calm
Van de Velde was born in Leyden where he was taught by his father, also a marine specialist. He was active in Amsterdam and, after 1672–3, in England, where, among his first pictures, was a set of marine overdoors (1673) at Ham House (National Trust).

Purchased for £1,675 by Mrs Greville from Agnew's in 1919.

34 Follower of AELBERT CUYP (1620–91)
The Maas in Winter with the Huis te Merwede
Probably a later pastiche of one of only two winter scenes by Cuyp, in the Earl of Yarborough's collection. Bought from Lesser as autograph for £2,625 by McEwan in 1894.

35 Attributed to PAULUS MOREELSE
(1571–1638)
An Unknown Woman
Moreelse worked in Utrecht, primarily as a portraitist. Bought by Mrs Greville in 1918 for £880.

36 AELBERT CUYP (1620–91)
A Landscape with a Herdsman and Bull
This pastoral scene (reminiscent of the Rhine valley) bathed in warm light is typical of the Ital-

A Landscape with a Herdsman and Bull; by Aelbert Cuyp (no. 36; Picture Corridor)

ianate landscapes painted by Cuyp (a native of Dordrecht) under the influence of the Utrecht artist Jan Both, who visited Italy *c.*1638–41. Probably painted in the 1650s, it was bought for £3,000 in 1919 by Mrs Greville from Colnaghi's.

37 After ÉLISABETH VIGÉE-LEBRUN (1755–1842)
Supposed portrait of Louis-Jean-Baptiste Vigée (1758–1820)
The artist's brother was a poet and secretary to the Comtesse de Provence. Mme Vigée-Lebrun was famous throughout Europe for her portraiture, and published her memoirs in 1835–7. The original is in the St Louis Art Museum.

38 Style of CAREL FABRITIUS (1622–54)
The Head of a Boy
Probably a 19th-century pastiche in the style of this pupil of Rembrandt, who was killed in the explosion of the Delft powder magazine in 1654. Bought by Mrs Greville from Agnew's in 1938.

39 NORTH ITALIAN, ? late 15th-century
? Giason del Maino (1435–1519)
A famous lawyer and a cousin and counsellor of Ludovico Sforza, Duke of Milan. Acquired in 1935 from Agnew's by Mrs Greville.

40 Attributed to the MASTER OF THE ST BARTHOLOMEW ALTARPIECE (active *c.*1470–1510)
Head of a Young Man
The artist derives his name from the triptych (1500–?1510) painted for St Columba, Cologne, now in the Alte Pinakothek, Munich. Painted *c.*1480; acquired by Mrs Greville in 1936 from Agnew's.

41 Attributed to ADRIAEN ISENBRANT (active early 16th century–d. 1551)
A Lady as the Magdalen
Isenbrant settled in Bruges in 1510, where he lived until his death; purchased from Agnew's in 1938.

42 Attributed to ISAAK LUTTICHUYS (1616–73)
An Unknown Woman

44 PIETER DE HOOCH (1629–84)
The Golf Players
Painted around 1660, it may represent the artist's children, Pieter (b. 1655) and Anna (b. 1656). Two larger versions include the artist's wife on the right. De Hooch's best pictures were painted in Delft before his move to Amsterdam in 1661, and are comparable to those of Vermeer. Bought by McEwan from Lesser in 1894.

45 LUDOLF BAKHUIZEN (1631–1708)
A States Yacht and Fishing Boats off a Jetty
A painter of portraits as well as landscapes, who for most of his life was based in Amsterdam where he became the leading marine artist after the departure of the van de Veldes to England in 1672. Bought from Lesser by McEwan in 1893.

46 Attributed to JACOMETTO VENEZIANO (active 1472–94)
An Unknown Woman
Thought to be a late work by this Venetian artist, who painted a saint (? St Mark) on the back of the panel, possibly so that it could be reversed and the portrait of the lady could be concealed. One of Mrs Greville's last purchases (in 1940 from Agnew's).

47 BERNARDO STROZZI (1581–1644)
A Venetian Gentleman
Mrs Greville's first recorded purchase of an Old Master picture (in 1916 for £650). Strozzi was sometimes called 'Il Prete Genovese' (the Genoese priest) on account of his place of birth and his years as a Capuchin friar. In about 1631, he left Genoa for Venice, where he remained for the rest of his life. This portrait was probably painted in the late 1630s; the costume is typical of Venice at that date.

48 WILLEM VAN DER VLIET (*c.*1584–1642)
An Unknown Boy of ten, 1634
Van der Vliet's portraits are sometimes confused with those of his nephew and pupil, Hendrick, who also worked in Delft. Bought in 1920 for £750 by Mrs Greville from Agnew's.

49 ADRIAEN VAN OSTADE (1610–85)
Peasants before a Fire, 1668
Of exceptional quality, this genre interior is typical of this prolific Haarlem painter's work. He also painted portraits and biblical scenes, as well as being an etcher and draughtsman. Bought from Agnew's for £2,887 in 1893 by McEwan.

50 GERARD TER BORCH (1617–81)
An Officer making his Bow to a Lady
The scene (painted around 1662) is probably intended to suggest an idealised brothel, and the old woman in the background, a procuress, but such scenes of life in fine settings were meant to be ambiguous. The fashionably dressed young lady may be an idealised portrait of the artist's sister, Gesina (1631–90). Bought by McEwan from Lesser in 1896 for £3,000.

An Officer making his Bow to a Lady; by Gerard ter Borch (no. 50; Picture Corridor)

51 GERARD TER BORCH (1617–81)
An Unknown Man
Painted *c.*1675 and bought by Mrs Greville through Borenius in 1922.

52 SALOMON VAN RUYSDAEL (1600/3–70)
An Estuary, 1647
Painted in the same year as no. 31 and purchased for £800 from Colnaghi's by Mrs Greville in 1920.

53 JACOB VAN RUISDAEL (1629/30–82)
The Zuider Zee Coast near Muiden
Ruisdael was a native of Haarlem who settled in Amsterdam after 1657, and was arguably the greatest of all 17th-century Dutch landscape painters. Painted *c.*1675, about the same time as and perhaps as a companion to the picture depicting the beach at Egmond-aan-Zee (of virtually identical size) in the National Gallery, London (no. 1390). Both paintings were sold in 1772 by the Duc de Choiseul (1719–85), one of the most discerning 18th-century French collectors of Dutch Old Masters. Bought by McEwan in 1893 from Agnew's.

54 JAN VAN DER HEYDEN (1637–1712)
The Church at Maarsen
Its pair is in the Berlin Museum; in both pictures, the figures are attributed to the specialist Adriaen van de Velde (1636–72). Maarsen is on the River Vecht, north of Utrecht. Bought by Mrs Greville after 1923.

55 JAN VAN GOYEN (1596–1656)
An Estuary, 1655
Van Goyen travelled widely and was extremely prolific both as a landscape painter and draughtsman (a landscape drawing is also at Polesden). His mature style is distinguished by a near-monochrome palette.

56 JAN VAN GOYEN (1596–1656)
The Beach at Scheveningen, 1648
Although the steeple does not conform precisely with that of the church at Scheveningen, it is probably this resort, just outside The Hague, that is represented here. Bought by Mrs Greville from Colnaghi's in 1920 for £1,800.

57 Attributed to CORNELIS DE MAN (1621–1706)
The Game of Cards
De Man was born and died in Delft, but he spent five years abroad, mainly in Italy. He was particularly fond of painting reflections in mirrors.

58 DAVID TENIERS the Younger (1610–90)
The Tric-Trac Players
An early work of *c.*1640, when the artist was influenced above all by Adriaen Brouwer (1605/6–38), the pioneering Flemish painter of genre scenes. From 1647 until 1656, Teniers was in the service of the Archduke Leopold Wilhelm, the Habsburg governor of the Spanish Netherlands, as curator of his magnificent collection of Italian Old Masters. One of three paintings by Teniers bought in 1894 from Lesser, for £3,150, by McEwan, who, as a brewer, may have been drawn to his tavern scenes.

58A DAVID TENIERS the Younger (1610–90)
The Alchemist
Also an early Antwerp work of the 1640s.

59 DAVID TENIERS the Younger (1610–90)
The Card Players
Probably painted *c.*1645. From 1763 to 1794 owned by one of the greatest 18th-century English connoisseurs, Sir Lawrence Dundas, 1st Bt, of Aske (*c.*1710–81).

60 FRANS VAN MIERIS the Elder (1635–81)
Self-portrait at the age of 32, 1667
Born and died in Leyden, where he was one of the most notable members of a group of *fijnschilders* (fine painters) whose exquisitely finished handling is exemplified by this self-portrait. His master, Gerard Dou (1613–75), the founder of this Leyden school, called him 'the Prince of his pupils'. His patrician demeanour and clothing in this portrait (and the book) suggest the nobility and learning of his profession. The pose derives from Titian's so-called *Portrait of Ariosto* (National Gallery), probably via Rembrandt's similar 1639 self-portrait etching and 1640 painting (National Gallery). Bought on Mrs Greville's behalf for £771 by Agnew's at Christie's in 1919. The elaborate neo-Rococo frame (*c.*1860) was presumably made for the owner of *The Times,* John Walter III (1818–94), who acquired the picture by 1857, and who rebuilt his house at Bear Wood, near Reading, in 1865–74 around a central top-lit picture gallery.

61 Attributed to GABRIEL METSU (1629–67)
A Head of a Negress
A possibly damaged fragment set into a later illusionistic surround. Metsu was another *fijnschilder,* a native of Leyden who lived in Amsterdam from 1657. Bought in 1922 by Mrs Greville through Borenius.

Self-portrait; by Frans van Mieris the Elder, 1667 (no. 60; Picture Corridor)

62 Attributed to the MASTER OF THE FEMALE HALF-LENGTHS (active first half of 16th century)
The Nativity
This anonymous master was active in Bruges or Antwerp. Bought by Mrs Greville, probably from Langton Douglas, *c.*1934.

63 JOHANNES LINGELBACH (1622–74)
A Group of Horsemen and Peasants
Lingelbach lived for most of his life in Amsterdam. A figure specialist, he was influenced by Philips Wouwermans. Purchased in 1893 for £210 by McEwan from Lesser.

114 QUIRINGH GERRITSZ. VAN BREKELENKAM (*c.*1620–67/8)
An Old Man sleeping by a Fireside attended by a Maidservant
The old man, having drunk a jug of wine, has fallen asleep by the fire while a maidservant looks on. A typical moralising genre scene by this Leyden painter, who entered the city's painters guild in 1648.

DRAWING

JAN VAN GOYEN (1596–1656)
The Ramparts at Dordrecht

SCULPTURE

The marble sarcophagus (or coffin) carved with a Bacchic procession of men, women, elephants, lions and leopards, and with winged lions at the sides, is Roman, 3rd-century AD. Sarcophagi of this type and date often had carved portraits of the deceased on the lid (missing here).

FURNITURE

EAST ARM OF CORRIDOR:

The black and gold japanned wall-clock, with painted dial inscribed 'R. Hardy, Newark', is *c.*1750–60.

The pair of giltwood stools covered in red damask is *c.*1730 (with later restorations) in the style of William Kent (1685–1748), one of the first English architects to design complete interiors, including furniture.

SOUTH ARM OF CORRIDOR, EAST END:

The walnut and marquetry longcase clock of *c.*1695 is inscribed on the dial 'Rob. Halsted. London'. Halsted's workshop was in Fleet Street.

The chest inlaid with marquetry of ivory, bone and various woods is north Italian, 19th-century. This style of marquetry is called *alla cestosina* from its supposed association with Carthusian monasteries, and derives from Arabic models, being practised in Venice and Lombardy.

The two oak 'Farthingale' upholstered chairs are English, *c.*1650.

The walnut chairs upholstered with 19th-century *gros point* needlework on a black ground (in mid-18th-century style) are French, *c.*1740 (apart from three similar chairs of *c.*1900).

SOUTH ARM OF CORRIDOR, CENTRE:

The four mahogany armchairs with low backs are probably Portuguese, *c.*1760, and are covered in contemporary needlework.

The pair of walnut and marquetry chests-of-drawers is north Italian, *c.*1720.

The set of high-backed walnut chairs with partially gilded splats and legs with pink damask upholstered seats is probably Portuguese, *c.*1710.

The set of oak Windsor chairs with interlaced arch-shaped backs is English, 19th-century, and was listed here in 1943.

WEST END OF CORRIDOR:

The four carved walnut chairs are French, *c.*1560, in the style of Jacques Androuet du Cerceau (*c.*1515–after 1584). Although heavily restored (probably in the late 19th century), their decoration is typical of the Italianate style of du Cerceau, who published numerous books of architectural and ornamental designs between 1549 and 1584.

The carved walnut table is French, *c.*1560, in the style of du Cerceau.

The elaborate cabinet on a Neo-classical giltwood stand is a mixture of interesting and early elements. Despite extensive restoration, it is essentially Franco-Flemish, *c.*1640, with earlier gilded and engraved fretwork applied to red velvet (some of it original) within ebony-framed panels. This engraved metalwork is extremely fine: around the cornice are hunting scenes, while the larger panels are oriental or classical in inspiration (the engraving in both styles is Flemish, late 16th-century). The large engraved panels on the sides of the cabinet are turned on their ends, so were clearly not designed specifically for their present locations. The marquetry and mirrored interior is typical of Flemish cabinets of this date. The piece is reminiscent of furniture by Pierre Gole (*c.*1620–84), a Dutchman who was Louis XIV's leading cabinetmaker from around 1656.

WEST ARM, EITHER SIDE OF SHOWCASE:

The set of four walnut chairs with seats and backs covered in needlework is English, *c.*1730. The upholstery is possibly original (the *petit point* central panels are certainly early 18th-century), but the *gros point* surrounds are partly late 19th-century, which could mean that the upholstery was applied to the chairs at this date.

Early Italian and Netherlandish pictures hang in the south-west corner of the Picture Corridor above 16th- and 17th-century French and Franco-Flemish furniture

PORCELAIN

EAST ARM WITHIN WINDOW EMBRASURES:

The pair of tall Mandarin vases and covers with leaf-shaped panels decorated in *famille rose* colours reserved within a mazarin blue ground is Chinese, Qianlong, *c.*1750.

ON RADIATOR COVERS:

The pair of Chinese export soup tureens and covers in the form of geese is Qianlong, *c.*1780.

SOUTH ARM, EAST END, IN SHOWCASE:

The showcase is one of three made *c.*1900, which were moved to Polesden from Charles Street after Mrs Greville's death. Within is a large gathering of Chinese porcelain decorated in the *famille verte* palette within panels reserved on a gilded powder-blue ground, Kangxi (*c.*1700–20).

ON RADIATOR COVER OPPOSITE DOOR TO LIBRARY, CENTRE:

The blue-and-white pear-shaped urn and cover with two handles is Chinese, Kangxi, *c.*1700. The silver spout is later.

EITHER SIDE:

The pair of blue-and-white egg-shaped jars and covers painted with panels of tree peonies issuing from rockwork is Chinese, Kangxi, *c.*1700.

SOUTH ARM, WITHIN WINDOW EMBRASURES:

The four (a set of three and one similar) tall Mandarin vases and covers painted in *famille rose* colours on giltwood stands of *c.*1890 are Chinese, Qianlong, *c.*1760.

ON RADIATOR COVERS AND ON FURNITURE:

This porcelain, of various types and palettes, is Chinese, predominantly of the Kangxi period (1662–1722).

SOUTH ARM, WEST END:

The large bell-shaped maiolica jardinière decorated with a coat of arms is Italian (Cantagalli), *c.*1875–1900.

WEST ARM, IN WINDOW EMBRASURES:

The pair of tall Mandarin vases and covers with leaf-shaped panels decorated with birds, rockwork and bamboo reserved within a mazarin blue and gilt ground is Chinese, Qianlong, *c.*1750.

A Chinese export soup tureen in the form of a goose, c.1780 (Picture Corridor)

SHOWCASE:

Within the French showcase (late 19th-century in the Louis XV style) is a catholic mixture of English and European porcelain, glass and enamel, including three large and six small plates decorated with flowers (in the style of the Zurich factory, late 19th-century); TOP SHELF: a pair of frill vases and covers (Bow, *c.*1765) and a single frill vase (Bow, *c.*1765); SECOND SHELF: a pair of frill vases (French, 19th-century, in the Derby style), two tankards (left, Nymphenburg, *c.*1770, and, right, Nymphenburg, 1771) and a *milchglass* decanter (Bohemia, *c.*1780); BOTTOM SHELF: a pair of enamel candlesticks (French, 19th-century, in the Bilston style).

CARPETS

The various runners and rugs will not always be in the same positions, and the Trust is gradually replacing the most vulnerable with copies. They are all Persian (Bidjar, Feraghan, Hamadan or Kirman).

THE LIBRARY

The Library remains almost exactly as it was designed for Mrs Greville by Mewès and Davis, apart from the replacement by copies (in 2000–1) of the original striped yellow satin curtains, and of a sofa and two easy chairs upholstered to match (sold in 1943). In 1943 it also contained a PYE television. According to the *North Mail and Newcastle Chronicle* (1934), this was Mrs Greville's favourite room: 'The white panelled walls are lined with books, and mirror doors are most attractive. A plain amber carpet [still in place] and deep comfortable chairs in yellow brocade give a most delightful effect of constant sunshine and the only other touch of colour comes from the odd pieces of blue and white china scattered about the room.' The *Sunday Times* mentioned 'great bowls filled with yellow gladioli', which complemented the 'bright buttercup yellow coverings for chairs and sofas'. The newspaper accounts agreed that Mewès and Davis had based the room on the designs of Louis-Rémy de la Fosse (c.1659–1726), a French architect active in Germany, where in 1706 he became court architect to the Elector of Hanover (crowned George I of Great Britain in 1714). The mirror-backed doors were something of a Mewès and Davis trademark, used extensively in the bedrooms at Polesden.

CHIMNEYPIECE

Given the French flavour of the room, it is curious that Mewès and Davis chose to introduce this English chimneypiece of c.1765. The central panel depicts Winter (putti building a fire for a shivering woman).

PICTURES

OVERMANTEL:

43 AELBERT CUYP (1620–91)
Portrait of a one-year-old Boy with a Sheep
The gold chain and medal suggest that this is a boy (both sexes wore skirts at this age). Recently rediscovered to be a rare early portrait by this Dordrecht painter, who is better known for his golden landscapes (see no. 36; Picture Corridor). It was painted in 1639, when Cuyp was only nineteen and still sometimes working with his father. Acquired from Agnew's in 1920 for £2,500.

LEFT:

100 GEORGE MANSON (1850–76)
A Girl with a Basket of Eggs, 1873
McEwan owned at least four works by this Dutch-influenced Edinburgh artist.

RIGHT:

101 GEORGE MANSON (1850–76)
A Child with a Porringer, 1874

ON TABLE:

119 GEORGE MANSON (1850–76)
Self-portrait, 1869

MINIATURES

IN TWO CASES ON CENTRAL TABLE:

Mrs Greville formed her collection mainly between 1891 and 1910, and the majority of the 40 miniatures was acquired from the London dealer Tessiers of Bond Street. They are displayed within two giltwood table cases on red damask, which she favoured as a foil for miniatures. The miniatures include excellent English and continental 17th-, 18th- and early 19th-century portraits by, or attributed to, Peter Cross (c.1645–1724; no. 12, c.1695), Christian Richter (1678–1732; no. 35, after c.1702); Jeremiah Meyer (1735–89; no. 24, c.1780); John Smart (1742/3–1811; nos. 36 and 37, 1773 and 1776), William Grimaldi (1751–1830; no. 20, 1806) and Andrew Plimer (1763–1837; nos. 32–4, 1807, c.1790–5 and c.1810).

FURNITURE

AT FIREPLACE END:

The large early 19th-century mahogany writing-table is covered with its original appurtenances, including the numerous framed photographs of Mrs Greville's guests remarked upon by the 1930s newspapers, 'all with signed inscriptions testifying to their friendship for this popular hostess'.

EITHER SIDE OF FIREPLACE:

The pair of wing chairs upholstered in needlework is English, c.1710. The central panels of *petit point* needlework depicting classical figures among trees are probably contemporary, as are the *gros point* surrounds, but their marriage is likely to have been arranged c.1900.

The smaller mahogany pole-screen is English, c.1750, and frames contemporary *petit point* needlework.

OPPOSITE WINDOWS, LEFT:

The pair of walnut armchairs with curved stretchers and upholstered in needlework is probably French, c.1685. The needlework, partly in chinoiserie style, is essentially c.1700 but it is likely that the *gros* and *petit point* upholstery was made up around 1900, when the tasselled fringes and antiquarian nailing were applied to this and the following pair.

The Library

The harlequin pair of walnut armchairs upholstered in needlework is c.1680, the backs incorporating similar *petit point* panels within *gros point* surrounds. The chair frames are probably Franco-Flemish.

WALL OPPOSITE FIREPLACE:

The tortoiseshell, ivory and ebony inlaid walnut coffer on stand, as the inscription records, was given to Mrs Greville in 1920 by her close friend Princess Victoria Eugénie (Ena), a granddaughter of Queen Victoria, who married Alfonso XIII of Spain in 1906 (they were almost killed by an anarchist's bomb thrown at the wedding procession). The coffer, also inlaid with engraved mother-of-pearl panels, is Spanish, *c.*1600. The walnut stand is modern.

WINDOW WALL:

The Pembroke tables of mahogany (left) and burr yew (right) inlaid with other woods are English, *c.*1780.

The single mahogany armchair is English, in the French style of *c.*1760, and is upholstered with needlework of *c.*1745.

The walnut armchair is Italian, *c.*1680. The needlework, incorporating a *petit point* panel depicting Pomona, Roman goddess of gardens, orchards and ripening fruit, is probably French, *c.*1700, and was presumably applied when the 17th-century-style fringes were applied around 1900.

CENTRE OF ROOM:

The mahogany writing-desk is English, *c.*1800, and supports a Louis XV *encrier* (a stand fitted with inkwells) in Chinese lacquer, ormolu and Chantilly porcelain, of *c.*1760.

The tortoiseshell, ivory and ebony inlaid walnut coffer in the Library was given to Mrs Greville by the Queen of Spain in 1920

The mahogany centre-table with frieze is English, *c.*1770.

CARPET

The rug is Persian (Kirman), second half of the 19th century.

PORCELAIN

ON CHIMNEYPIECE:

The garniture of five fluted two-handled porcelain jars and covers, surmounted by figures of Shishi (Buddhistic lions) and painted in Imari colours with gilding, is Japanese, *c.*1700.

ABOVE BOOKCASES:

The blue-and-white porcelain is Chinese, predominantly of the Kangxi period (1662–1722), and was placed above the bookcases by Mrs Greville.

EITHER SIDE OF DOORS:

The two pairs of large blue-and-white porcelain jars and later covers are Chinese, Kangxi, *c.*1690. In 17th-century Europe such jars were coveted status symbols, and were sometimes provided with special wooden stands (as at Petworth and Hampton Court).

THE LOBBY

PICTURE

97 GEORGE PAUL CHALMERS, RSA (1836–78)
The Young Cavalier, 1860
Chalmers was one of a group of Scottish artists who were influenced by Sir David Wilkie and by Dutch Old Masters. This picture probably belongs to McEwan's earliest phase as a collector.

FURNITURE

The small mahogany and satinwood cabinet with glazed upper section and cylinder-front screening shelves is French, *c.*1780, and was listed here in 1943.

CLOCK

The longcase clock, with silvered dial inscribed 'John Payne London' (1731–95), is *c.*1760.

THE STUDY

The Study and adjoining lavatory (door in south-west corner – not open, pending restoration) were added by Mewès and Davis as a private sanctum for Mrs Greville (her bedroom suite was above). The décor was apparently faithfully renewed after the 1960 fire, and the pale yellow and cream damask curtains are original (albeit cut down). The 'mauve pile carpet', as it was described in 1943, was also replaced *c.*1960 and copied for a second time in 1995. Mewès and Davis designed the fireplace so that the view south across the valley could still be appreciated (the flue runs up to one side), and, in the evening, sliding mirrors fill up the window embrasure.

PAST FURNISHINGS

As in the Library, there were originally 'two stuffed armchairs' upholstered to match the curtains, and several other useful pieces of furniture were also sold in 1943, including a damask-covered invalid's chair (Mrs Greville became increasingly immobile towards the end of her life). The walls were hung with 18th- and early 19th-century English mezzotints, all sold in 1943 (but similar prints have recently been hung). None the less, the majority of the present furniture was listed here in 1943.

MINIATURES

ON DESK IN BOW WINDOW:

The miniatures of William McEwan, Helen Anderson, Ronald Greville (Mrs Greville's father, mother and husband) are all by Eunice Patterson (active 1900–14) of Market Harborough, Leicestershire. They were probably commissioned by Mrs Greville, and were cased by Tessiers.

FURNITURE

LEFT OF ENTRANCE DOOR:

The mahogany barometer is English, c.1760.

IN FRONT OF FIREPLACE:

The rosewood games table is English, c.1790. The 18th-century Indian chess set given by Queen Mary to Mrs Greville was listed here in 1943.

TO RIGHT OF FIREPLACE:

The mahogany fire-screen incorporating a panel of contemporary needlework is English, c.1755.

BOW WINDOW WALL:

The pair of kingwood marble-topped commodes with ormolu mounts and enamelled handle plates is French, Louis XVI, c.1780. The grey and white marble tops are not original. The commodes are traditionally said to have been supplied by Joseph Duveen (1869–1939), the most famous dealer of his day.

IN THE BOW WINDOW:

The mahogany writing-desk is English, c.1800, of 'Carlton House' form, named after Carlton House, Pall Mall, the London home of the future George IV.

The four armchairs upholstered in striped yellow silk in the Louis XVI style were probably designed by Mewès and Davis and are identical to chairs made by Waring & Gillow for Mewès and Davis's Ritz Hotel, Piccadilly (1904–5).

METALWORK

ON CARLTON HOUSE DESK:

The pair of black and gold lacquer tea canisters is Japanese, 19th-century, and was given to Mrs Greville by Queen Mary for Christmas 1919.

CARPET

The silk rug is Persian (possibly Herez), c.1850.

PORCELAIN

The glazed showcase contains 18th-century Meissen and Fürstenberg porcelain including pieces from Meissen tea, coffee and chocolate services (no. 80, c.1725; no. 91, c.1730; and no. 92, c.1735) painted with wharf and chinoiserie scenes in the style of J. G. Herold (1696–1775), the dominant painter of the Meissen factory from 1720; and a Meissen yellow-ground cream jug (no. 84, c.1735)

A Fürstenberg porcelain tea-caddy, c.1770 (Study)

painted with military scenes after battle pictures by Georg Philipp Rugendas I (1662–1742), an Augsburg artist who studied in Italy. The rare Fürstenberg tea and coffee service (no. 79, c.1770) is painted with *singeries* (monkeys engaged in human pursuits), probably by C. G. Albert.

THE SALOON

Mrs Davis-Thomas, the daughter of Mrs Greville's architect Arthur Davis (joint-partner in Mewès and Davis), remembers that her father was asked to design a room 'fit to entertain Maharajahs in'. He provided an extravagantly carved and panelled *salone* of c.1700 removed *en bloc* from an Italian *palazzo*, complete with painted canvases let into the ceiling. The panelling, probably supplied by White, Allom & Co., was cut to fit. The numerous spare pieces stored in the Polesden cellars confirm that the cream, blue and gilded decoration is original (albeit repainted in 1960 after the fire). Sadly, the 'rich crimson Spitalfields brocade', shown in early photographs and originally woven for William McEwan's Edinburgh house, was replaced inaccurately in 1960 (the pattern is different, and the curtains no longer have tasselled tie-backs, nor are there velvet inner curtains). The marble fireplaces, in the French style of c.1730 (of a type widely installed by Mewès and Davis) and the herringbone parquet floor, almost hidden by Persian carpets, completed the extravagant ensemble.

Beverley Nichols thought the room was 'really quite appalling – over-gilt, over-velveted, over-mirrored like an extremely expensive bordel'. It was here, he remembered, that tea was served when there were large parties of weekend guests. One weekend in 1937, before the other guests had arrived, he recorded *verbatim* tea-time conversation in the Saloon between himself, Sacheverell Sitwell and Mrs Greville:

The poisoned darts were soon flying in all directions.
MAGGIE: Now I never say unkind things about people. Have you ever heard me say an unkind thing about anybody, Twenty-five [her nickname for Beverley Nichols]?
MYSELF (gulping): Never.
MAGGIE: But if anybody says anything unpleasant to me, I always make the same reply. I always say 'Thank you so much for telling me that. And next time I hear anything unpleasant about you, which I

expect will be very soon, I shall be sure to repeat it to you.' Why are you smiling, Sachy?...

PANELLING

The provenance of the panelling is unknown, but it is probably Italian, c.1700. The exotic style of the carving (for example, the cornice brackets) suggests south Italy.

CEILING PAINTINGS

Around the border of the ceiling and over the doors are rectangular canvases of putti holding garlands of flowers, while the roundels at the four corners depict incidents from the life of David recorded in the Old Testament. In the south-east corner (by the window), David refuses Saul's offer of armour and a sword before facing Goliath as he had 'not proved *them*' (Samuel I, 17, v. 38–9); in the north-west corner (by the left-hand door) Saul, jealous of David's victory, hurls a spear at him (Samuel I, 18, v. 10–11); in the north-east corner (by the right-hand door) David is given 'hallowed bread' by the priest, Ahimelech (Samuel I, 21, v. 2–6); in the south-west corner (by the window), Abigail lays gifts before David to make amends for her husband's insults (Samuel I, 25). Fire-damage to some of these scenes (see p. 5) makes them difficult to assess, but they would appear to be by the Neapolitan follower of Luca Giordano, Paolo de Matteis (1662–1728), which fits with the apparently south Italian provenance of their setting.

PAST FURNISHINGS

The *Onlooker* in 1910 described the Saloon as 'a beautiful apartment modelled mainly on a gallery in [a] villa of the Italian Renaissance'. This impression would have been all the greater before the Italian furnishings were sold in 1943 and replaced by the French furniture previously in Charles Street. The Italian furniture (late 17th- and 18th-century, or modern copies) included a large gilt-wood console table, two small shield-shaped mirrors in gilt frames and three Italian armchairs upholstered in dark red cut velvet. This was supplemented by an eclectic mixture of stuffed armchairs, French furniture (predominantly Louis XV and XVI, but including a large mirror in Louis XIV style), Japanese lacquer cabinets and ornaments, an ebonised Steinway boudoir grand piano, as well as many of the present furnishings. The floor was

The Saloon

covered with five Persian runners (laid parallel to the end walls) and four Persian carpets all combining dark blue and red, the predominant colours of the upholstery; the curtains were of red and gold brocade.

PICTURES

CENTRE:

29 HERMAN SCHMIECHEN (b. 1855; active in London 1880–95)
Margaret Anderson, the Hon. Mrs Ronald Greville, DBE (1863–1942)
Signed and dated *89* or *99*
For biography, see no. 1 (Picture Corridor). In Mrs Greville's day, the portrait hung in the Morning Room at Charles Street. Schmiechen had an international career, including painting German relatives for Queen Victoria.

LEFT AND RIGHT:

26, 27 Follower of JEAN-BAPTISTE MONNOYER (1636–99)
Flowers in a China Vase
These two pictures hung in the Breakfast Room at Charles Street.

FURNITURE

WALL OPPOSITE WINDOWS, CENTRE:

The bombé commode of kingwood inlaid with marquetry, elaborately mounted in ormolu, and with a Breccia marble top, is French, Louis XV, *c.*1750. It is stamped by Jacques-Philippe Carel (active *c.*1723–*c.*1760; *maître* 1754) and is consistent with his style (cf. a similar commode in the Frick Collection, New York). The commode also bears the stamp of Denis Genty (*maître* 1754; active until 1770), an *ébéniste* who also acted as a dealer. His stamp probably indicates either that he repaired the commode or that it passed through his hands (although it is not impossible that he, rather than Carel, made the piece). One of the ormolu mounts is said to bear on the back the signature of Jacques Caffieri (1675–1735), one of the most famous exponents of the Rococo style, who was *fondeur-ciseleur* (founder-chaser) to Louis XV, and they are certainly in his style.

WINDOW WALL, LEFT:

The marquetry break-front commode on cabriole legs, mounted in ormolu, and with circular ormolu handles on the three drawers is French, Louis XV, *c.*1775. The top is of Rouge Royale marble.

The set of six giltwood armchairs (fauteuils à la reine) upholstered in contemporary tapestry is French, Louis XV, *c.*1760. This type of chair was copied widely in England at the time.

CENTRE:

The small ormolu-mounted bombé commode, veneered with kingwood, inlaid with floral marquetry and with a Breccia marble top, is French, Louis XV,

*c.*1750. It is stamped by Pierre Roussel (1723–82; *maître* 1745).

RIGHT:

The ormolu-mounted break-front commode, with Greek-key frieze, cabriole legs, Breccia marble top and inlaid with chinoiserie scenes in marquetry, is French, *c.*1770–5. The marquetry and the ormolu mounts are of high quality, and although the piece is unstamped, it is very similar (in particular the distinctive arched ormolu centrepiece) to signed commodes by the German Parisian *ébéniste* Christophe Wolff (1720–95; *maître* 1755).

CENTRE OF ROOM, EAST END:

The large ormolu-mounted writing-desk (bureau plat), set with panels of tulip-wood, cross-banded and veneered à *quatre faces*, is French, Louis XV, *c.*1760.

WEST END:

The small ormolu-mounted writing-desk of kingwood inlaid with marquetry is French, Louis XV, *c.*1760.

CARPETS

The large carpet and flanking rugs are Persian, first half of the 20th century, of Bidjar type, the central field with a Herati design on dark blue.

The French commode, c.1770–5, in the Saloon is inlaid with chinoiserie scenes in marquetry

CLOCKS, BAROMETERS AND CHIMNEYPIECE ORNAMENTS

EAST END, ON CHIMNEYPIECE:

The ormolu clock surmounted by a putto as Apollo with an enamel dial inscribed 'Lefaucheur A Paris', is French, Louis XV, *c.*1750–60. The movement is modern. Alexandre Le Faucheur was clockmaker to Louis XV.

The pair of bronze and ormolu candelabra supported by four chained blackamoors is French, Louis XV, *c.*1770.

The pair of porcelain figures of cranes is Chinese, Qianlong (1736–95), with Louis XVI ormolu mounts.

RIGHT OF FIREPLACE:

The carved giltwood wall-clock with enamelled dial is French, Louis XV, *c.*1750.

BETWEEN WINDOWS:

The matching barometer and thermometer in parcel-gilt circular cases are French, inscribed 'Cappy & Mossy'. The thermometer is dated 1776.

WEST END, ON CHIMNEYPIECE:

The ormolu clock decorated with putti and a cockerel with an enamel dial inscribed 'Gille Lainé Paris' and supported on a *griotte* marble base is French, Louis XV, *c.*1770.

The pair of jasper urns and covers mounted in ormolu is French, Louis XVI, *c.*1775. The ormolu mounts are reminiscent of mounts by Pierre Gouthière (1732–1813/14).

PORCELAIN AND OBJECTS OF VERTU

WINDOW WALL:

The three cisterns or goldfish bowls on late 19th-century giltwood stands are French, Samson factory, 19th-century, in the Chinese *famille rose* style of the Qianlong period, *c.*1750.

WINDOW WALL, ON COMMODES:

The pair of large octagonal vases and covers in Imari colours is Japanese, *c.*1700.

WALL OPPOSITE WINDOWS:

The pair of Mandarin jars and covers on late 19th-century giltwood stands is Chinese, Qianlong (1736–95).

(Right) A brown jasper owl on a silver gilt perch, attributed to Carl Fabergé (Saloon)

SHOWCASES

END WALLS: EAST WALL, LEFT OF FIREPLACE:

This late 19th-century Louis XVI-style case (one of a pair) contains Chinese *famille verte* enamelled on the biscuit figures of the Kangxi period (1662–1722).

RIGHT OF FIREPLACE:

Apart from the group of a man with a buffalo (no. 203, top left), which is possibly 19th-century, and the group of Chenwu, Supreme Lord of the Dark Heaven, flanked by attendants (no. 204, bottom left), which may be slightly earlier (ie late Ming), all the pieces date from the Kangxi period (1662–1722).

WEST WALL, LEFT OF FIREPLACE BY WINDOW:

This late 19th-century showcase in Louis XVI style (one of a pair) contains, on the whole, mid- to late 18th-century and other European porcelain:
TOP SHELF: The figures are Meissen, *c.*1750–65, as is the late 19th-century scent bottle in the form of a boy (no. 180) (the other, in the form of Columbine, no. 181, is English 'Girl-in-a-Swing' porcelain, *c.*1755). SECOND SHELF: A Meissen *Shepherd* and

Shepherdess (nos. 184a and b), *c*.1755, flank a pair of Bow candlesticks emblematic of Winter and Spring (nos. 186a and b), *c*.1765. THIRD SHELF: The figures and groups are English: (at either end) a pair (nos. 188a and b) of Derby sweetmeat figures, *c*.1765–70; a Chelsea/Derby *Bagpipe Player*, *c*.1775 (no. 190) and two Bow groups: *a Hen and Chicks*, *c*.1760 (no. 192) and a *Shepherdess*, *c*.1765 (no. 191). BOTTOM SHELF: *A pair of Nymphenburg saucers*, *c*.1765 (nos. 193a and b), flanks a Sèvres cooler for two decanters (*seau à compartiments*). It is dated 1773, but was probably decorated in the early 19th century.

RIGHT OF FIREPLACE:

TOP SHELF: (At either end) a pair of Plymouth or Bristol figures of putti personifying Autumn, *c*.1770 (nos. 165a and b); a pair of German late 19th-century scent bottles (nos. 169a and b); and a Rococo Longton Hall vase, painted by the 'trembly rose' painter, *c*.1755–60 (no. 166). SECOND AND THIRD SHELVES: A set of four Derby figures emblematic of the Seasons, *c*.1765 (nos. 167a, b, c and d) and two mid- to late 19th-century Meissen groups of putti (nos. 170 and 173). BOTTOM SHELF: Flanking one of a pair of Sèvres coolers for two decanters, 1773 (see above), are two companion Meissen figures of street vendors, both modelled by Kändler and Reinicke, one *c*.1755, the other *c*.1770 (nos. 174 and 175).

WALL OPPOSITE WINDOW, LEFT:

The 19th-century ormolu-mounted kingwood showcase in Louis XV style (one of a pair) contains numerous figures, groups, vases, bowls and other useful wares which are (with one exception) Chinese of the Kangxi period (1662–1722), or slightly earlier, decorated mostly in *famille verte* colours. In the centre of the top shelf is a Japanese Arita porcelain insect cage and stand, pierced and enamelled in colours, *c*.1720 (no. 226), presented to Mrs Greville at Christmas 1920 by Queen Mary.

RIGHT:

This showcase contains a variety of Chinese porcelain, jade and soapstone figures, groups and other miscellaneous items dating mainly from the late Ming (*c*.1600–44) and Kangxi periods (1662–1722) with a few later pieces of the Qianlong period (1736–95). There is also a figure of a pheasant (no. 157), apparently Chinese, mid-18th-century,

but in fact a 19th-century imitation by Samson (Paris).

There are four table showcases in the centre of the room.

IN FRONT OF FIREPLACE (EAST END):

The 19th-century French showcase in the Neo-classical Louis XVI style contains:

The toilet service in its original case with a dressing mirror within the lid is French (Paris), *c*.1795. The silver-gilt instruments have mother-of-pearl handles. The showcase also contains an early 19th-century French toilet set in a tortoiseshell case, and four rat-tailed English silver spoons (1683–96).

WEST END, IN FRONT OF FIREPLACE:

The 19th-century French table showcase of kingwood mounted with ormolu in Louis XV style contains a miscellany of objects of vertu made of various semi-precious stones, sometimes set with jewels. The majority are Chinese (small vases, bowls, bottles and figures in jade, agate and other hardstones), predominantly 18th- and 19th-centuries. There are also numerous carved figures of animals and birds, inspired by such Chinese and Japanese pieces, attributed to Carl Fabergé (1846–1920) and Louis-François Cartier (1818–1904), and made around 1900.

CENTRE OF ROOM:

The pair of 19th-century French Louis XVI-style table showcases with ormolu supports and mounts in the manner of Adam Weisweiler (1744–1820; *maître* 1778) contains a variety of *bibelots, objets d'art* and porcelain.

TOWARDS WALL OPPOSITE WINDOWS:

Around the perimeter of the case are late 17th- and 18th-century Chinese porcelain tea-cups and saucers in *famille rose* or *famille noire* colours. In the centre are decorative Chinese objects fashioned from soapstone, rock crystal, agate, jade and jadeite, including snuff bottles (nos. 8 and 9) and a writing-brush washer (no. 11).

WINDOW SIDE:

The second showcase in the centre of the room contains European objects of vertu and jewellery. Around the perimeter are several decorative boxes and snuffboxes, most of which are German, *c*.1750–60; the others include a Louis XV tortoiseshell

The Tea Room

THE TEA ROOM

snuffbox with piqué gilt scrollwork (no. 32), a shell-shaped box of Canton enamel (no. 27), a fine *Directoire* enamel box (no. 18) and an oval tortoiseshell snuffbox with Edward VII's cipher on the lid, given to Mrs Greville in 1909. In the centre of the bottom row is a rectangular bell-push by Cartier in the form of an obsidian owl's head with diamond eyes set on a rose quartz base (no. 79). This was presumably used by Mrs Greville on the Dining Room table. The other items include presents from Edward VII, decorated with his cipher.

Designed by Mewès and Davis for Mrs Greville, *c.*1906–9, and possibly executed under the direction of White, Allom & Co., in a somewhat etiolated version of the Louis XVI style of *c.*1785. The panels incorporate a series of late 18th-century pastoral landscapes based on mid-18th-century French models by artists such as Fragonard and Boucher. The re-creation of such rooms was popular among Mrs Greville's contemporaries. The Frick Collection, New York, contains a room designed *c.*1913–16 by Sir Charles Allom to incorporate a series of pastoral subjects by Fragonard.

Despite its name, the Tea Room was not used exclusively at tea-time (the Saloon catered for large parties), but it certainly provided an appropriate setting for more intimate gatherings.

PICTURES

DUTCH or FLEMISH, late 18th-century
Eight Pastoral Landscapes
These fanciful and bucolic scenes have figures in the style of such 18th-century French painters as François Boucher, in Italianate settings, but are more probably Flemish or Dutch, by someone in the circle of decorative painters like the Dutchman Jurriaan Andriessen (1742–1819), who ended up producing wallpaper.

PAST FURNISHINGS

Almost all the original furniture listed in the 1943 inventory was subsequently sold. It was predominantly French and gilded. The upholstery of the 'gilt settee and four fauteuils, of Louis XVI design' was 'striped cream silk with flower sprays in riband work'. This corresponded (as did the 'flowered cream silk brocade' of a gilt armchair) with the 'Three pairs of cream silk curtains' at the windows (they were replaced by a different material soon after the Second World War and again in 1960, although the trimmings were reused). Otherwise, there was a 'stuffed settee and two armchairs, upholstered in green damask', four small gilt chairs, and rather incongruously a 'nest of three red lacquer tables', as well as various chinoiserie or Japanesque ornaments.

FURNITURE

ON CHIMNEYPIECE:

The ormolu mantel clock surmounted by putti as Cupid and Psyche is signed by Jean-Baptiste du Teitre, a Parisian clockmaker (recorded 1715–42). The movement is modern.

RIGHT OF FIREPLACE:

The dwarf carved giltwood four-leaf screen with panels of Aubusson tapestry is French, Louis XVI, *c.*1780.

CENTRE OF ROOM:

The pair of small giltwood sofas covered in tapestry, *c.*1780, is of a type known as *confidents* or *tête à têtes* because of their small size. They are in the style of Georges Jacob (1739–1814; *maître* 1765), a specialist chair maker and a pioneer of the Neo-classical style, who received numerous royal commissions.

(Right) The pastoral landscapes in the Tea Room were inspired by 18th-century French artists such as Boucher

The oval writing-table with ormolu gallery, channelled frieze and inlaid with mahogany is stamped by Jean Demoulin (1715–98; *maître* Paris *c.*1745, *maître* Dijon 1780). It is a *table à écrire* or *table-éscritoire*, a writing-table designed for women and usually fitted with a drawer for writing materials and a writing slide and side platform (as here).

AROUND THE ROOM:

There are numerous pieces of French Louis XV and XVI furniture (*c.*1760–90) including (right of window on far wall) a Louis XV dressing-table (called a *coiffeuse* or *table de toilette*), typically arranged with a folding central mirror surrounded by compartments and small drawers; a Louis XVI satinwood roll-top writing-table (*bureau à cylindre*) with mirrored doors above, *c.*1785 and (centre of room) a small writing-table (*bureau de dame*), Louis XV, *c.*1760, shown open to reveal its interior of drawers.

CARPET

The carpet with a dark blue field is an Indian late 19th-century 'jail' carpet made in Jaipur or Agra.

SCULPTURE

JULIE CHARPENTIER (active 1787–d. 1843)
Portrait of a Woman
Terracotta, 1788
This may represent the sculptor's younger sister, a bust of whom she exhibited in 1787.

SILVER

RIGHT OF FAR WINDOW (ON DRESSING-TABLE):

The boxed tea-set incorporates a pair of caddies (by Samuel Taylor, 1770) and a sugar vase (1763) within a silver-mounted rosewood box by Reily and Storer, 1840. Another English silver tea caddy is dated 1726.

RIGHT OF FAR WINDOW (ON LOUIS XVI TABLE):

The silver teapot on stand is by Marshall & Sons, and is engraved with McEwan's initials.

CENTRE OF ROOM, LEFT (ON LOUIS XVI TABLE):

The salver on trumpet foot is by Samuel Hood, London, 1698 (with later armorials).

BELOW:

The oval cake basket with pierced sides and decorated in the Rococo style is by John Luff, London, 1741.

RIGHT (ON LOUIS XV/XVI MARBLE-TOPPED TABLE):

The large salver on four feet is hallmarked London, 1770 and is engraved with the arms of Richard and Elizabeth Day of Hawleigh, Suffolk, who were married in December 1770.

The silver teapots are English, early 18th-century. The smaller round one is probably by John Fawdery, London, 1729; the larger is by Gabriel Sleath, London, 1717.

BELOW:

The unusual cake basket in the form of a scallop shell is by Phillips Garden, London, 1750.

THE BILLIARD ROOM

This room was created by Poynter in 1903–5, and left virtually unchanged by Mewès and Davis, who confined themselves to bringing in a new fireplace of *c.*1800 and altering the doorcases and alcove surrounds.

PAST FURNISHINGS

The Billiard Room was designed and furnished as a male sanctum, with Smoking Room and Gun Room beyond. The square part of the room around the fireplace was furnished like a gentlemen's club library with books, easy chairs and writing-tables. In the main rectangular section stood a mahogany-framed billiard-table by Burroughs and Watts, sold in 1943 (the present table is also by Burroughs and Watts and was brought in from the former employees' social club in the stables). The room was probably painted green, given that the curtains (now faded to brown) and the upholstery were green (damask or leather). The strips of carpet around the billiard-table, and a square carpet in the rest of the room were all of 'arabesque design with green ground', matching the carpet that still survives in the Gun Room, which was also laid with a 'blue felt surround'. The lamps above the billiard-table had green silk shades, and the big sofa and armchair for spectators were covered in green damask. The walls were hung with 19th-century coloured engravings by Henry Alken and his contemporaries (all sold in 1943) of typical fox-hunting, coaching and racing scenes.

PICTURES

93 WALTER WILLIAM OULESS, RA (1848–1933)
William McEwan (1827–1913), 1901
For biography, see no. 4, p. 13. Originally hung in the dining-room at Charles Street. Ouless was a prolific and immensely successful society portraitist.

92 SAMUEL BOUGH, RSA (1822–78)
The Port of London, 1863

95 ANTON MAUVE (1838–88)
A Scanty Meal: Snow Scene with Flock of Sheep
Bought by McEwan for 160 guineas in 1877, it was hanging in the Dining Room by 1910. Mauve belonged to the Hague School, which was particularly popular in Scotland in the late 19th century.

117 Sir WILLIAM MCTAGGART, RSA (1835–1910)
Seascape, 1877
Bought by McEwan, and characteristic of his early purchases, which were primarily of works by fellow Scots.

118 Sir WILLIAM MCTAGGART, RSA (1835–1910)
The Pleasures of Hope, 1860
A rare early work in oils.

152 H. G. HINE (1811–95)
Moorland Landscape, 1891

FURNITURE

OVER CHIMNEYPIECE:

The oval gilded mirror and flanking mirrored sconces are among the original furnishings of the room, and were possibly designed by Mewès and Davis.

CERAMICS

The turquoise and black faience plates are Persian, possibly 17th-century.

The turquoise and black faience bowl is Persian, 13th–14th-century.

CLOCK

The ormolu wall-clock is French, early 19th-century, in the style of *c*.1730, by Jean Corrier (active 1772–1812).

THE SMOKING ROOM

The Smoking Room is now arranged as a family museum, displaying photographs and memorabilia of Mrs Greville's occupation of Polesden Lacey. As can be seen from numerous photographs of Mrs Greville's house parties, the male guests (and indeed their host, Ronnie Greville) were seldom separated

The Billiard Room in 1923

from tobacco out of doors, but indoors it was considered impolite to smoke anywhere other than a separate room of this kind (except in the Dining Room after dinner, and that was an innovation of Edward VII's). The King was fond of cigars and Turkish cigarettes, which became widely fashionable as a result. By the 1920s, and previously in racier circles, smoking indoors was increasingly tolerated, and the use of special smoking-rooms became less obligatory. Women, too, gradually became *aficionados* of the weed. Today, the wheel has come full circle, and Victorian attitudes to tobacco again prevail.

PAST FURNISHINGS

The present wallpaper and curtains date from *c*.1980. The original wall colour is unknown, but the overall colour scheme of the curtains, upholstery and carpet was based on red. The curtains were of red velvet with matching velvet pelmets; the carpet was of a floral design on a red ground with a similar rug (presumably a hearth rug), while a 'blue felt surround' covered the floorboards; and the upholstery was either red leather or 'woolwork' (on a mahogany sofa and five chairs in Hepplewhite style). The walls were hung with English Edwardian landscape and portrait mezzotints, mainly after 18th-century painters such as Gainsborough, Reynolds, Hoppner and Raeburn.

PICTURE

94 REGINALD PARNELL
The Hon. Mrs Ronald Greville (1863–1942), 1904

FURNITURE

The gilt convex mirror surmounted by an eagle is English, *c*.1830. It and the Edwardian chandelier are the only pieces surviving from Mrs Greville's time.

IN CENTRAL SHOWCASE:

The Polesden Lacey visitors' book was originally in the Entrance Hall. The first signature (in 1907) is Edward VII's.

THE GUN ROOM

Presumably for the storage and preparation of guns for game shooting, the Gun Room was very sparsely furnished in 1943, containing 'A Flemish oak cupboard, with carved frieze', a 'mahogany oval table . . . An invalid's chair, a wicker armchair, an umbrella stand; and two circular pouffes'. The present carpet (*en suite* with that originally in the Billiard Room) originally had blue felt surround masking the floorboards. The walls were hung with 24 coloured engravings of steeplechasing, stag-hunting, fox-hunting and coaching scenes.

TAPESTRY

The tapestry, inspired by the paintings of David Teniers the Younger (1610–90), is Flemish, *c*.1750, and is probably from the workshop of Pieter van den Hecke. It was originally part of a larger set.

THE STABLE COURTYARD

Originally constructed as the 'Stables and Coach House' by Cubitt for Joseph Bonsor between 1821 and 1823, it was almost entirely rebuilt (1903–5) by Poynter for Sir Clinton Dawkins. Poynter's water tower, in Italian quattrocento style, dominates the entrance between a coach house and a 'Motor House' or garage. The north range (to the right) with a cast from the Parthenon frieze beneath a central pediment, housed stables and a harness room. During Mrs Greville's time, the extent of the stabling was reduced to provide room for a bailiff's office and the staff social club, which was provided with a full-size billiard-table (see p. 39). The west range of the courtyard (opposite the entrance arch; now the shop) was a hay and corn store with a mess room and accommodation for grooms (and later also for Mrs Greville's golf professional). The houses on the south side of the courtyard were for other members of staff. To the west of the courtyard, in a separate building, Poynter built an 'Engine House', which supplied the house and estate buildings with electricity.

41

THE GARDEN, PARK AND ESTATE

Occupying the high ground between Bookham Common to the north and Ranmore Common to the south, Polesden has always been noted for its commanding views. In 1801, James Edwards (the author of *A Companion from London to Brighthelmstone*) described the house's position:

In an eminence with a lawn on the acclivity of the hill, from whence you have a diversified prospect to the south of a deep vale which terminates at a small distance by the rising hills covered by venerable beech woods, and the fertile vale consisting of a beautiful assemblage of trees, fields and cottages, composes an agreeable scene. A narrow prospect through the vale to the east [towards Box Hill] is very extensive.

In 1803 the diarist Joseph Farington called this view 'a peep of beautiful distance'. The statesman and playwright Richard Brinsley Sheridan, who lived at Polesden from 1797 to 1816, thought it 'the nicest place, within a prudent distance of town, in England'. Today, standing on the terrace and looking south over the parkland in the valley towards the wooded hills of Ranmore, it seems all the more remarkable that Hyde Park Corner is less than 25 miles away.

There is mention of 'the garden at Polesdene' in 1333–4, but few other records of the estate before the 18th century. The early 18th-century accounts mention repairs to outbuildings, such as 'the Pa[r]tridge room' [ie a game larder], and to equipment such as nets for catching partridges and larks. This suggests that Polesden was by then a reasonably self-sufficient small agricultural and sporting estate. Catching, shooting and fattening game was clearly an important element of Polesden life, judging by references to such things as: 'fixing up a Gunn rack in the Kitchen and mending a Gun', and 'the Coops to Fatten Fowls etc and to keep

(Left) The Rose Garden

Pa[r]tridges'. Nor was the gardening establishment neglected: partitioned 'Drawers etc' were provided for 'the Gardeners Seeds', and a 'Form to Stand on for to cut Trees' was also made.

The earliest indication that there was a garden of some size is given by John Rocque's map in 1768. This shows the Carolean house with a walled formal garden to the north on the site of the present Walnut Lawn and what appear to be walled gardens to the south, with a long terrace to the south-east, presumably the subsequently extended Long Walk overlooking the valley. The creation of this spectacular terrace has traditionally been credited to Admiral Sir Francis Geary, who bought Polesden in 1747, but it is possible that its origins are connected with the ownership of Arthur Moore (1723–9) or of his relations, who sold Polesden to Geary. Moore was a great builder, whose gardens at nearby Fetcham Park were 'adorned with Canals, Basons...', and terrace gardening is generally associated with the early rather than the mid-18th century. Geary probably repaired or extended the terrace (the date 1761 is cut into its masonry), and it was extended from 900 feet (its length in 1804) to 1,300 feet 'under the direction of Mrs Sheridan' (ie between 1804 and 1816). The 1797/8 map indicates that by his death in 1796, Geary had removed the walled gardens shown in 1768, and that the garden plan had become more informal, as one would expect.

Beneath the terrace, the landscape was gradually emparked and, by the 1818 survey, both the valley and the area to the east of the house bordered by the Admiral's and Nun's Walks were designated as parkland. The 1818 and 1842 maps show that the principal garden was, as today, west of the house, and this is likely to have been the site of Sheridan's rose garden (which prompted his invitation to a beautiful guest: 'Won't you come into the garden?

I would like my roses to see you'). A newspaper report of Sheridan's harvest celebrations in October 1802 strikes an appropriately bucolic note:

A large tent was erected on the lawn, capable of accommodating three hundred persons, who were treated with English cheer and ancient hospitality, and the industrious and deserving girls of character were rewarded each by an harvest present from their amiable hostess. A select party dined at the mansion house, which was enlivened by the vivacity and gaiety of Mr Sheridan, and the peasantry departed, after preserving the utmost regularity, order and decorum, at a proper hour, all filled with gratitude for their hospitable and kind reception.

THE 19TH CENTURY

The garden improvements put in train by Sheridan's successor, Joseph Bonsor, were probably also to the west of the house. In 1803 Farington noted of Polesden that Sheridan's 'characteristic neglect is seen all about it – everything manifesting disorder'. In 1818 Bonsor paid a Mr Jopling to undertake estate and garden repairs, including the 'Garden Wall ... nearly all new' for £600, the 'Greenhouse entirely new' for £650 and the building of 'Garden sheds with Fire Places' and a new 'Melon Ground'. In 1818 too there is mention of £800-worth of work covering 'New Plantations, Garden, Orchards, & planting Trees in every vacancy', and 'Mr. Ettershank the Nurseryman' was paid for the cost of 'Plants and Labour' in 'planting the Garden, and the Orchard'. Bonsor enlarged the estate (as had Admiral Geary) and paid '£8 per Acre' on the 'general improvement of the Land' between 1818 and 1824. His renovations were all embracing (encompassing the purchase of livestock, improving the water supply by 'making new Tank Ponds, [and] erecting Pumps' and renewing the 'Farming utensils, viz waggons, carts, Ploughs, Rollers, Harrows etc'). The park was grazed by a flock of sheep that was enlarged by Bonsor, who also purchased cattle, including Alderney cows to provide milk, horses, pigs and other beasts. The water supply had traditionally depended upon wells and dew-ponds and, given the eminence of the house and the lack of a river in the valley, Bonsor's installation of tanks and pumping equipment was clearly an essential improvement. In 1824 and 1825 Bonsor calculated

The valley to the south of the house was open parkland in the early 19th century

The terrace below the house was divided into formal beds;
photograph taken about 1900

that he had planted 20,000 trees – a 'Covered Saw
Pit' implies that this was, in part at least, a commer-
cial enterprise. His son, also Joseph, expanded the
estate to 916 acres (nearly three times the acreage in
1818), but in 1853 sold it to Sir Walter Farquhar.
The reason for selling an estate into which so much
money had been poured is unknown but, given the
family's undoubted financial acumen, it may have
been connected with the decline in the timber
market after 1850.

On the previously open lawn to the south of the
house, Farquhar laid out a rectangular formal
garden split into smaller compartments with a
fountain centred on the south façade of the house.
Immediately to the south-west at the western end of
the Long Walk was a Fernery linked to the walled
gardens to the west of the house by a strip of woodland separating (as it still does) the garden beneath
the south front and the large lawn below the walled
garden. The 1870/81 Ordnance Survey map shows
that Farquhar extended the Bonsors' walled garden
(on the present site) and formalised the planting. By

this time, the walled garden was no longer separated from the west side of the house by a road leading down to the valley: partly on the line of the old
road, there were now walks through woodland
around what had become a pleasure ground encir-
cling the west lawn.

MRS GREVILLE

Farquhar died in 1900, and Polesden was acquired
in 1902 by Sir Clinton Dawkins, whose major alterations to the house (1903–5, to the design of
Ambrose Poynter) seem not to have been paralleled
in the garden, judging by his preservation of
Farquhar's formal fountain parterre beneath the
south front. Poynter's proposal to extend this
terrace garden southwards was unexecuted. Mr and
Mrs Greville, who bought the house in 1906, also
toyed with the idea of extending Farquhar's parterre southwards to the Long Walk. An elaborate
scheme descending on five levels to the parkland in
the valley was one of two similar proposals drawn
up in 1907 by Frank Stuart Murray of Durand,
Murray & Seddon. In 17th-century style, with a

wealth of clipped hedges and topiary, the parterres were to be centred on a bow-fronted *perron* flanked by a vast semicircular pergola. Murray also produced designs for other parts of the garden, but although none was executed, reminiscences of his ideas were adopted: in the rose pergolas of the walled garden, in the rounded yews of the eastern forecourt, in the square and semicircular bastions of the eastern end of the Long Walk. By 1912, Mrs Greville had turned her attention to the area south of the walled garden, commissioning R. Wallace & Co. of Colchester to provide designs for a formal layout incorporating a fountain and a croquet lawn, which were again left unexecuted. Part of a 'Proposed Rock and Water Garden', designed by Pulham & Co., survives from about this time, but it was never finished due to difficulties with the contractors.

By contrast to her speedy and decisive elaboration of the house, Mrs Greville's treatment of the garden was apparently hesitant and unresolved. Even so, by 1914 the essentials of the garden layout shown in photographs of the 1920s seem already to have been carried out. Having shelved her more radical schemes, she settled upon a revision of what she found. To some extent this was a simplification. She dismantled Farquhar's formal parterre on the south front, while retaining the central fountain, but by 1948 (and probably within her lifetime) the whole area had reverted to lawn. Similarly, she preserved the west lawn as an open space, opening up a vista towards the south front of the house and confining her horticultural attentions to the walled garden. The spaciousness of the lawns relates more naturally to the parkland beyond than extensive formal parterres would have done. This impression was enhanced until the Great Storm of 1987 by the flanking canopies of mature trees planted in the 19th century, which Mrs Greville supplemented by inviting visiting royalties to plant specimen trees as mementoes of their visits (a practice inaugurated by Edward VII in 1909, and revived by the Prince of Wales in 1988). A degree of formality is provided by the urns in 17th-century French style, which flank the south front, and by the marble, lead and terracotta statues and ornaments elsewhere, which serve to punctuate the vistas or provide centrepieces

for compartments of the walled garden. These were presumably designed or supplied by Mewès and Davis or their subcontractors.

Within the walled garden, Mrs Greville seems to have preserved the Victorian plan of four compartments, although it is likely that she installed the rose pergola, originally provided with a central dome. By 1916, she had extended the walled garden westwards, building a new section of brick wall on the south side which incorporated north-facing 'pockets for plants'. Against this wall on the south, she also extended the long border. The gravel path was originally flanked by a second border on the edge of the west lawn, but this was removed by the National Trust, when it became too expensive to maintain. At the same time the elaborate and much taller plantings in the remaining border against the wall were thinned and simplified. The 1920s photographs indicate how these and other elements of Mrs Greville's garden have been diminished to the detriment of their original style and grandeur. Mrs Greville's western extension of the garden continued beyond the bridge over the sunken road (Yew Tree Lane). Planted as an orchard about 1975, it was originally a vegetable garden, the vegetables screened by flower-beds flanking the central path leading to the summer-house at the far end.

The Trust's long-term intention is to restore the original elements of Mrs Greville's garden (and the earlier features that she incorporated). This will, of course, have to be undertaken in a spirit of pragmatism because the present staff of five gardeners is considerably smaller than her complement of fifteen. However, it should be feasible to achieve a much more faithful representation of a great hostess's garden, designed, like the house, for the recreation of distinguished and sophisticated guests. Their amusement was catered for in other ways. A golf course was laid out by 1909 within the park to the north and east of the house. Golf was extremely fashionable in the years before the Great War, and the Polesden course was used by Edward VII and by George VI and the Queen Mother during their honeymoon in 1923. Tennis was also popular – there were hard courts alongside the avenue leading up to the Stable Block and grass courts were set up on the west lawn. The plantations and woodland

The Herbaceous Border in July

The Polesden garden staff about 1928

were carefully husbanded as game preserves – the valley admirably lent itself to the challenge of high-flying pheasant and partridge. As in earlier times, there were herds of cattle and flocks of sheep, and Polesden was self-sufficient in most produce, as the surviving estate accounts (for 1915–18) reveal.

Henry Smith (head gardener, 1938–64) remembered that 30 tons of coke were burned annually to force vegetables and fruit in the hot-houses. Flowers were produced under glass in May and afterwards were grown outdoors. Mrs Greville was particularly fond of violets and lily of the valley. Violets had to be produced in November, which was achieved by bringing the crowns into cold frames in August. The busiest week of the year was Royal Ascot, when about 20 guests would be staying and, including the staff, up to 75 people had to

be fed. Sprays of flowers to match the ladies' dresses and white or red carnations for buttonholes were provided each day. Flowers, vegetables, milk, butter and fruit were sent up to London daily, at first by train and subsequently by van. There was a large staff. Between 1908 and Mrs Greville's death in 1942, the fifteen gardeners worked a 52-hour week from 6am to 6pm, with breaks for breakfast and lunch. As well as the gardeners (who doubled as caddies on the golf course), there were teams of woodmen, handymen, chauffeurs and mechanics.

In February 1938 Mrs Greville conducted Henry Smith's interview for the head gardener's post from her bed and declared: 'Smith, I want you to speak to me as if I were a man.' She asked him 'to concentrate on growing things suitable for the English climate', as her foreign friends were used to exotic plants and envied her lawns and roses.

POLESDEN BEFORE
MRS GREVILLE

Polesden Lacey is famous for its art collection and as an archetypal Edwardian house where Edward VII, his descendants and a host of foreign royalties mingled with Society as the guests of one of the most distinguished of all hostesses, Mrs Ronnie Greville. Its history goes back much further, however.

The name 'Polesden' is Saxon, and the earliest recorded owner was one Herbert de Polesden, who was selling land here in 1198. The 'Lacey' suffix probably derives from the family of John Lacy, who owned Polesden in 1387–93, but it is first described as 'Pollisdon Lacy' only in 1562. There has been a house here since at least 1336. In 1630 Anthony Rous acquired the estate and shortly afterwards completely rebuilt the medieval house, placing the date '1631' above the main entrance on the east side. Polesden descended in the Rous family until 1723, when it was bought by Arthur Moore (1666?–1730), a notable economist and politician, seated at nearby Fetcham Park, which was built by William Talman around 1700. Moore was a self-

made man, Lord Commissioner of trade and plantations (1710), MP, director of the South Sea Company, Comptroller of Army Accounts (1704), an expert on commerce, whose 'profusion consumed all' in his private life. In 1729 he sold Polesden to his brother, Thomas Moore (1668–1735), a soldier who was made paymaster of land forces abroad in August 1713, and whose monument by Thomas Carter in Great Bookham church portrays him in Roman military dress. Thomas Moore left Polesden to his brother's son William, MP for Banbury, who commissioned James Stedman to add a west wing and octagonal pavilion to the south front in 1735–48. The payments to Stedman (Bodleian Library, MS North *c*.62, f1–47) reveal that Polesden was a reasonably substantial building, incorporating a 'Great Stair Case', a 'Great Room', two galleries, a first-floor room 'at S.E. Corner where the Family Pictures are', a Library with glazed bookcases, a 'China Room', 'Octagon Room' and a full complement of additional reception rooms, bedrooms and

The entrance front as rebuilt by Anthony Rous in 1631; engraving after a drawing by J. Herne, 1809

49

servants' quarters. Stedman's improvements included repairing furniture and extended to the purely utilitarian ('making a Horse to dry Cloaths on', 'making a stool for the Dairy Maid' and 'making a frame to Strain the Jelly through').

William Moore died in 1746, leaving debts which his executors settled by selling Polesden for £5,500 in 1747 to Francis Geary (1710?–96), a naval captain of Welsh descent, then serving with the Channel fleet under Sir Edward Hawke. Geary was a friend of Hawke (who privately entreated him 'to watch those fellows [the French] as close as a cat watches a mouse'), and also of Admiral Edward Boscawen, the hero of the battles of Louisberg and Lagos Bay, and his neighbour at Hatchlands. Like Hawke and Boscawen, Geary rose to the rank of Admiral (in 1775), but his career, though distinguished, was not marked by famous victories. In 1780, due to weak health, he resigned his command of the Channel fleet, was created a baronet in 1782, and spent fourteen years of honourable retirement at Polesden. His second son, Sir William Geary, inherited but soon moved to his mother's estate in Kent, where he was elected MP for the county.

Polesden was leased to Richard Brinsley Sheridan (1751–1816), whose trustees bought it for £12,384 in 1797 (although the purchase was not completed until 1804) with the benefit of his second wife's dowry of £8,000. Sheridan adored Polesden, rejoicing in his role as a country squire, giving lavish entertainments to his friends and to the local populace, wanting to 'see real justice done to the cottages and poorest claimants', buying 'two great china jars' for the dairy, and writing to a friend with 'a hatful of Polesden violets on the Table ... and three samples of Lambs wool'. He regarded Poles-

(Left) Thomas Moore (1668–1735), who bought Polesden from his brother in 1729; monument by Thomas Carter in Great Bookham church

(Right) Richard Brinsley Sheridan (1751–1816); by Sir Joshua Reynolds, 1789 (private collection)

den as a haven from the hurly-burly of his life in London, where he shone in Parliament as an orator and at Drury Lane as a dramatist and theatre manager. He was both a generous friend and landlord, but his extravagance, and that of his second wife, put him at the mercy of his creditors. In 1798 his expenditure on Polesden was criticised by his stage manager at Drury Lane: 'Foreboding of bankruptcy, such things as wood and canvas not to be had, yet three thousand guineas given for an estate.' After the burning of Drury Lane Theatre in 1809, his financial affairs became even more involved, and he was also dogged by ill health, partly caused by his long-standing love of drink. When he was forced to let Polesden, some of his numerous friends (who included the Prince Regent, Charles James Fox, the Duke of Wellington and Lord Byron) lent him a house near Leatherhead so that he could stay in touch with his farm and estate. He had many schemes for Polesden and, according to the topographer J. P. Neale (1824): 'About the year 1814, Mr Sheridan began to pull down the old Mansion, designing to rebuild it on a large and magnificent scale; but his protracted illness, and other reasons, caused his plans to be abandoned, and from that time the house, being uninhabitable, became a heap

of ruins, and the grounds totally neglected.' He and his wife did, however, extend the Long Walk and probably began the process of landscaping the valley beneath the house.

In 1818, two years after his death, Polesden and its 316 acres were bought for £10,000 by Joseph Bonsor (1768–1835), a stationer and bookseller from a Lincolnshire landowning family, who demolished the remains of the house and commissioned Thomas Cubitt to replace it in the Neoclassical style. Cubitt was the most prominent of a family of builders and is best known for his development of Belgravia and Pimlico in London and Kemp Town at Brighton. Polesden, built in 1821–3 at a cost of £7,600, was typical of Cubitt's plain, substantial but rather uninteresting style. Bonsor also paid Cubitt to build lodges, stables and a coachhouse as well as to undertake general repairs. Cubitt supplied 'Furniture viz Bookcases, Glasses, Marble Slabs, etc.'; other furniture was provided by Dowbiggin & Co. and by Messrs Snell, who were paid no less than £1,600. China and glass were supplied by Davenport & Co., and papering and decorating were done by Robson and Hale. Bonsor's rental book (1818–26) reveals that he laid out nearly £50,000 on these and other Polesden

The entrance front as rebuilt by Thomas Cubitt for Joseph Bonsor in 1821–3

*The Saloon c.1900, when Polesden belonged to Sir Walter
Farquhar*

acquisitions and renovations. Bonsor's son Joseph
succeeded his father in 1835 and sold the estate in
1853.

The new owner was Sir Walter Farquhar, Bt
(1810–1900), of an old Ayrshire family, whose
grandfather, the 1st baronet, was physician to the
Prince Regent. Farquhar was a prominent advocate
of teetotalism and a correspondent of Gladstone.
He extended the house (1853–70), but the sole
evidence for this is provided by survey maps. Sir
Walter's son sold Polesden in 1902 to Sir Clinton
Dawkins (1859–1905), a civil servant, banker and
expert on Egyptian and Indian financial affairs. In
1903–5, Dawkins's architect, Ambrose Poynter,
son of the painter Sir Edward Poynter, PRA,
extended the six-bay front of the 'ugly and incon-
venient' house by two bays, preserving only 'some

rooms and a portico on the south front'. The rooms
'were made into a suite comprising a large and small
drawing room and a library' (the present Saloon,
Tea Room and Library). Cubitt's central pavilion of
four bays with its portico of Ionic columns was
preserved with a minor change to the ground-floor
windows and with the addition of a balustrade and
pediment at roof level. The west, east and north
fronts were completely rebuilt around a central
courtyard and, like the south front, remain virtually
intact today (as does the internal layout), even after
Mrs Greville's additions in similar style of c.1906–9.
She also preserved the colour of Poynter's building,
which was 'plastered externally with yellowish
stucco, the window frames and cement dressings . . .
painted white . . . with a green slate roof'. Poynter's
Times obituary expressed regret that he did not
produce 'a single work on such a scale as to leave
permanent proof of his undoubted genius'. Polesden Lacey remains a rare memorial.

EDWARDIAN POLESDEN

'Maggie Greville! I would sooner have an open sewer in my drawing room', declared Lady Leslie. To Cecil Beaton she was 'a galumphing, greedy, snobbish old toad who watered at the chops at the sight of royalty . . . and did nothing for anybody but the rich'. Her tongue, 'as sharp as a needle', could certainly 'be dipped in gall' and she plunged her 'little fountain pen filler into pots of oily venom', which she generally squirted at women, 'for she had few enemies among men'. According to Osbert Sitwell, her enemies 'enchanted her, for she was a courageous and an accomplished warrior, and liked to be able to make use of her technique, acquired through many years. Thus when she entered an assembly, many a fashionable hostess quailed.' There was, however, another side to her, for she was much loved by her friends for her hospitality, kindness and her 'skilfully malicious' wit. A.J. Balfour (Prime Minister, 1902–5) described her conversation as 'a sort of honeyed poison'. Lord Boothby thought she 'was a bit of an old bag, but very good to me'. Childless herself, she adored and was adored by the young, and by a multitude of little dogs, which she buried in their own grave-yard. According to her goddaughter, Sonia Keppel:

[She] resembled a small Chinese idol with eyes that blinked. . . . In any generation, Maggie would have been outstanding. The daughter of a shrewd old Scottish brewer, from her earliest years she had taken an interest in his business, mastering the intricacies of its processes and management until eventually she won for herself a seat on the Board through her own business acumen. Always, she loved power, in her youth sipping it in small draughts, in her father's office in Edinburgh; later (with his money behind her), savouring it, in its social context, in the drawing rooms of Europe.

By the exclusive standards of the day, her mercantile Scottish background did not justify her undoubted snobbery. She was a collector of royalties who 'loved the great because they were great' and who 'liked to fill her house with celebrated and beautiful people', but her candour about her origins was refreshing: 'I'd rather be a beeress than a peeress', she stoutly exclaimed. She was indeed her own woman, despising pretentiousness and pomposity above all: 'If the point had been reached where a bubble had to be pricked, no one could perform the operation with a more delicate skill and, indeed, virtuosity.' She was intelligent, if not well read ('My dear, I know I'm not an educated woman'), and, as the daughter of a collector, was well informed about art.

The surviving images of Mrs Greville's beloved father, William McEwan (1827–1913), show him in old age, with a long spade-cut white beard, 'so thin . . . as to look almost transparent', as Lady Sitwell described him. He was born in Alloa, Clackmannanshire, on 16 July 1827, the third child of a reasonably prosperous ship-owner who died when he was four. His maternal grandparents paid for his education at Alloa Academy, and by the age of sixteen, he was a clerk at the Alloa Coal Company. By 1845 he was working in Glasgow where on his low wages he found it 'almost impossible to keep up the semblance of respectability and being at the same time ground down with labour'. He still found time to attend historical lectures at Glasgow University and to admire Shakespeare (and Shakespearean actresses) at the theatre. He has been rightly described as a 'great self-improver', who drew up reading lists (from Shakespeare and Milton to an *Etiquette for Gentlemen* via *The Wealth of Nations*) with the 'vague notion of making myself an intelligent man, which has always since my earliest years haunted me more or less'.

In 1847, on his departure from Glasgow, he was given an excellent reference by his 'mean, . . .

The Hon. Mrs Ronald Greville;
painted by Carolus-Duran at the
time of her marriage in 1891
(no. 1; Picture Corridor)

abusive and humiliating' employer: '[McEwan] is a person of the most strict probity, integrity and steadiness and possesses an excellent knowledge of accounts'. The hard road to riches can be traced in the meticulous records of his personal expenditure, which already included gifts to charity. He was abstemious and, curiously for a brewer, seems to have briefly flirted with teetotalism – in 1850 subscribing to the Huddersfield Total Abstinence Society (a far cry from the sybaritic world of Mrs Greville).

After his move to Edinburgh in 1851, he immersed himself in the practicalities of brewing as a trainee in his uncle John Jeffrey's brewery. In 1856, with the encouragement of his brother-in-law James Younger (whose Edinburgh brewery was founded in 1749) and with £2,000 partly loaned by his mother, McEwan established the Fountain-bridge brewery in Edinburgh, soon to become famous for its McEwan's Export and India Pale Ale, the favourite beers of the British Army, brewed to withstand transport to the farthest flung outposts of the Empire. By the 1860s, he was exporting beers to India, the Antipodes, the West Indies and South America. By 1871, the 43-year-old McEwan employed 149 men and 53 boys, and by 1880 the business was valued at about £1m. He devoted much of his wealth to collecting pictures (see p. 61) and to philanthropy. He made the single largest financial donation to Edinburgh University (£115,000 to build a graduation hall, 1889–97), as well as presenting two portraits by Frans Hals and a Rembrandt to the National Gallery of Scotland. He was also MP for the Central Division of Edinburgh (1886–1900) and was made a Privy Councillor in 1907 after declining a peerage.

The precise circumstances of Margaret Helen Greville's birth are unknown, but the likely truth can be pieced together. She was rumoured to have been William McEwan's illegitimate daughter by Helen Anderson, a widowed Edinburgh lodging house keeper and whom he married in London in 1885. In 1943 Margaret, Marchioness of Crewe (a close friend who attended Mrs Greville's private burial at Polesden Lacey) declared that Mrs Greville's mother 'was the wife of the day-porter at Mr. MEwan's [sic] brewery. McEwan "for conve-

William McEwan; by Benjamin Constant, 1900 (no. 4; Dining Room)

nience" put him on night duty.' Something of the kind is probably true. Mrs Greville's death certificate states that she was 75 on 15 September 1942, but her birth certificate shows that she was born in London on 20 December 1863, and was actually three years older. There is no doubt that Helen Anderson (1836–1906) was her mother, but although William Anderson is stated to have been Mrs Greville's father on her birth and marriage certificates and although occasionally she was referred to as 'the step-daughter of a wealthy Scots brewer', it seems certain that Mrs Greville was really McEwan's natural daughter. Mrs Greville knew her true parentage: Polesden Lacey was left to the National Trust 'in memory of my father The Right Honourable William McEwan', and close friends like Osbert Sitwell also considered McEwan to be her natural father. Although, as a rich brewery owner, McEwan was well placed to hush up his liaison with the wife of an employee, it appears that the citizens of Edinburgh were too strait-laced to forget the impropriety. This probably explains why Mrs Greville was born in London and why her father and mother were later married quietly there, even though a new house in Palmerston Place, Edinburgh, was completed soon afterwards. Mrs Greville never forgave Edinburgh and 'Edinburgh society, when it visited London, felt the razor-sharp edge of her displeasure'.

Mrs Greville revered her father, hanging his portraits by Benjamin Constant and Walter Ouless in her dining-rooms at Polesden Lacey and Charles Street. From 1908 until his death in 1913, McEwan lived with his daughter, and photographs of her house parties show that he was virtually a permanent fixture long before. Osbert Sitwell records her touching concern for the old man:

[He] still insisted, though he had been knocked down more than once in the traffic, on walking everywhere by himself. He enjoyed these rambles, and to have insisted on someone accompanying him would have meant a painful admission, a lowering of dignity in his own eyes: so his daughter thought out an ingenious scheme. She engaged a private detective whose job it was for several years to see old Mr McEwan, without his being aware of it, safely over the dangerous crossings.

How she met Ronald Greville and was propelled into the heart of the Prince of Wales's Marlborough House set remains a mystery, but her father is said to have 'got Edward VII out of financial jams', and McEwan's great wealth certainly underpinned her social position. While there are numerous anecdotal records of Mrs Greville (and to a much lesser extent of her husband and father) after her marriage, the evidence for her *entrée* into London drawing-rooms is tantalisingly non-existent. Ronald Greville himself is a rather shadowy figure, despite his close friendship with the future Edward VII and with George Keppel, whose wife, Alice, was one of the senior and most delightful royal mistresses. His mother, Lady Violet Greville, daughter of the 4th Duke of Montrose and wife of the 2nd Lord Greville, only mentions him once in her memoirs to say that he was 'a great favourite of the late King Edward', was fond of steeplechasing and 'rode

many races before his premature end'. At the time of their marriage in 1891, Ronald Greville was a 26-year-old Lieutenant in the 1st Life Guards (his father's regiment), Maggie was 24, and the newly married couple moved into 4 Chesterfield Gardens, a fashionable Mayfair address conveniently close to McEwan's house at 16 Charles Street. Later, they moved to 11 Charles Street, and McEwan also provided a country seat for them: Reigate Priory, near Reigate, which was rented while Polesden Lacey was being restored (c.1906–9). Ronald Greville looks out from the numerous photographs of their royal house parties through heavy-lidded eyes, always with a cigarette in his gloved hands. The suave, somewhat dandified and enigmatic figure seems not entirely in tune with his 'awesomely dull' reputation. The daughter of his

The Hon. Ronald Greville

greatest friend, George Keppel, described him as 'a charming unambitious man', whom Maggie 'moulded affectionately into any shape she pleased'. Perhaps this explains his determined victory in a very difficult and close-run by-election in 1896, when he retained the East Bradford seat for the Conservatives against the Liberal Alfred Billson and the Labour candidate, Keir Hardie. Maggie then set herself the task of 'firmly conducting Ronnie through the lobbies of politics until two years before his death, in 1908'. Although he reigned at Polesden for only two years, he was a popular landlord, described by one of his tenants as 'genial' and 'kindly'. According to the *Sunday Times*, he was 'witty, good-natured, typically Irish'. One feels that his wife, who certainly had wit in greater measure, could not have been as fond of a dullard, even one who held the golden key to royal circles. Their marriage was extremely happy, only clouded by their inability to produce children. George Keppel said that she 'was devoted to Ronnie and that, had they had children, she would have given up much of her social life to be with them'.

In 1905 she was already described as 'one of the leading hostesses in London', who 'often had the honour of entertaining King Edward at dinner at her house in Charles Street'. In 1897 Mrs Greville (though apparently not Ronald) had been a guest at arguably the most exclusive and famous of all Victorian entertainments: the Devonshire House fancy dress ball, in celebration of the Queen's Diamond Jubilee. The guests (and their costumes) are recorded in a book of photographs (a copy with autographs is in the Polesden Library): Margaret Greville (as Mary Seaton) was in the procession of Queen Elizabeth I, which made a grand entrance at the opening of the ball.

For someone with ambitions to shine in Edwardian high society, the combination of a large town house and a country house within easy reach of the capital was desirable. Polesden was ideally situated and in good condition after its recent rebuilding by Ambrose Poynter and therefore required only internal embellishment and minor extension. The setting was even better, as the *Liverpool Courier* enthused on 7 June 1909: 'His Majesty enjoyed today from the windows of his suite of rooms at Polesden

Lacey a view over the beautiful Dorking valley, which is unsurpassed in Surrey.' The architecture of Polesden was attractive and undemonstrative, lending itself admirably to the erection of a new private wing to the left of the main entrance, which made the forecourt grandly symmetrical. The interior was spacious but plain, the layout (with a double-height entrance-hall-cum-sitting-room, for example) already corresponded to Edwardian ideas of convenience. All that was required, apart from even more bedrooms, bathrooms and dressing-rooms, was the opulent transformation of Clinton Dawkins's somewhat ascetic interiors.

Mrs Greville's architects, the Belgian Charles Frédéric Mewès (known to his employees as 'le Patron') and his much younger English partner, Arthur Davis, were eminently qualified to provide

The Louis XVI-style staircase hall at Luton Hoo was designed and built by Mrs Greville's architects, Mewès and Davis, in 1903–7

The ceiling of the Picture Corridor was inspired by the Jacobean plasterwork in the Long Gallery at Chastleton in Oxfordshire

their client with a setting worthy of her epicurean entertainments. With the triumphant successes of the Paris (1897–8) and London (1904–5) Ritzes behind them, and with Arthur Davis established in London as the English representative of the Parisian firm, Mewès and Davis had already made their mark in English commissions for both town and country houses. Their grounding in the classical Beaux-Arts tradition gave them the edge on most English architects in providing designs in the then supremely fashionable *tous les Louis*, but predominantly Louis XVI, style. Much of their work at Charles Street and at Polesden is typical of their interpretation of French 17th- and 18th-century architecture, as seen more exotically and on a much grander scale at the Ritz and at Luton Hoo, Bedfordshire (altered 1903–7 for Sir Julius Werner). The comparison extends to the fittings: chandeliers, sconces, marble fireplaces, firebacks, pokers and tongs, ormolu door furniture, marble-topped sinks, capacious baths on marble platforms, mosaic bathroom murals, flooring and so on.

Arthur Davis became a favourite of Mrs Greville, for whom he even designed a golden toothbrush (sadly no longer extant). Despite his youth (he was 28 when commissioned by Mr and Mrs Greville),

Davis was an assured performer. After winning gold medals at the Ecole des Beaux Arts (like Mewès under the tutelage of Jean-Louis Pascal), he was made a partner by the already well-established Mewès in 1900. The Mewès firm was international, an uncommon phenomenon at the time, with representatives in Germany, Spain and South America, as well as England. Like Mewès (who came from Alsace), Davis was Jewish, the cosmopolitan son of an English businessman, who was born in London and brought up in Brussels and Paris. He was bilingual in French and English (Mewès's limited command of the language cramped his style when in England). Davis was an urbane figure, as Sir John Betjeman noted in 1928: 'He was in pinstripe city clothes ... My overall impression is of amiability and smoothness when all was tweeds and rough rusticity.' By this time, his style was already old-fashioned. But Mrs Greville was delighted with his work, writing in 1915, 'I do not think it would be possible to find an architect more courteous, obliging and clever than you'.

His achievement at Polesden was to render the interior much grander and more comfortable, with an eye both to the reception of guests and to the display of pictures and works of art. Working with

59

Arthur Davis as a subcontractor was Charles Allom, knighted in 1913 for his work in the royal palaces, a colourful figure whose firm, White, Allom & Co., specialised in the re-creation of 'period' interiors. Allom himself was a notable cricketer and golfer, whose offshore racing yachts were famous. Like Arthur Davis, his clients included many of Mrs Greville's friends in aristocratic and royal circles, and White, Allom & Co.'s practice was also international: J. Randolph Hearst, the Californian newspaper baron and model for Citizen Kane, employed the company in the transformation of the medieval St Donat's Castle, Glamorgan, in the 1920s. For Hearst, Allom provided whole medieval buildings as well as 18th-century English furniture of impeccable provenance for, among other interiors, the bedroom of Hearst's mistress, the film star Marion Davies. At Polesden, his main contribution (in terms of design) appears to have been the Picture Corridor, which was given a 'Jacobean' barrel vault copied from the Long Gallery at Chastleton, Oxfordshire, by the plasterers Jackson's of London (a firm used by Robert Adam in the 18th century and often associated with White, Allom & Co.).

The late 18th-century marble chimneypiece in the Dining Room was probably supplied to Mrs Greville by the decorators White, Allom & Co.

White, Allom & Co.'s principal contribution seems to have been providing architectural salvage: the panelling of the Picture Corridor, of the palatial Saloon and (definitely) the Wren altar screen in the Central Hall. White, Allom probably also supplied the English late 18th-century statuary marble chimneypieces in the Dining Room and Library, which are of superb quality and, one suspects, too grand to have been made originally for Polesden; and, perhaps, much of the garden statuary and *objets trouvés* such as the Byzantine and trecento Italian wellheads and stoups (rose garden, central courtyard, forecourt and Entrance Hall). Mewès and Davis are known to have used several interior decorators (such as the fashionable Parisian Marcel Boulanger) and London decorators-cum-cabinetmakers like Waring & Gillow, Lenygon & Morant and Charles Mellier & Co. The last had already worked for the Grevilles at 11 Charles Street (in 1892), and Lenygon & Morant were later employed at 16 Charles Street (1913–14). Such firms would certainly have provided modern furniture, predominantly for bedrooms, such as King Edward VII's bed – one of the few items of bedroom furniture to survive, but also for the Saloon and Dining Room. The comfortably upholstered French and Italian-style armchairs once in the Saloon, and the gilt sideboards and lacquer dining-table formerly in the Dining Room were modern utilitarian elements in otherwise authentic groupings of antique furniture. Most of these Edwardian and later pieces were sold by the National Trust in 1943. Among the few survivals are the Louis XVI-style chairs now upholstered in striped yellow silk (Study), which were almost certainly designed by Mewès and Davis and made by Waring & Gillow, which supplied identical chairs for the London Ritz. Such a firm would also have been able to provide the silk upholstery and curtains described in the inventories, but which have largely disappeared from the showrooms and are now being re-created by the National Trust. The eclecticism of the interior is typical of Edwardian taste: it was perfectly normal, as at Polesden Lacey, to move from the Jacobean to the Stuart to the Georgian via Italy and France. The achievement of Mewès and Davis and of White, Allom & Co. is to have made such transitions appear so natural.

THE COLLECTIONS

Polesden and Charles Street were intended to offer a suitably luxurious setting for Mrs Greville's collections, which were considerable. From her father, she inherited an important group of paintings and a passion for collecting. William McEwan visited Chatsworth in the 1850s and shared his brother's enthusiasm for art, visiting Holland with him to look at pictures. His first recorded acquisition was in 1885, when his domestic insurance premiums already covered paintings. The 1885 purchase was both spectacular and philanthropic: the donation of Frans Hals's *Dutch Lady* and *Dutch Gentleman* to the National Gallery of Scotland. By this time, McEwan had already served on the committee of the fund-raising Fine Art Loan Exhibition (1878) at the Corporation Galleries in Glasgow, and given his special interest in Dutch pictures, he felt that the Scottish National Gallery should represent the finest 17th-century Dutch painters. In 1892, he presented the Gallery with its first (and only) Rembrandt – *A Woman in Bed*, for which he paid £5,775.

At Polesden Lacey today, there are thirteen Dutch Old Masters known to have been bought by William McEwan. In 1893 he bought the first seven: five landscapes, by van der Neer (no. 30), Salomon van Ruysdael (no. 31), Bakhuizen (no. 45), Jacob van Ruisdael (no. 53) and Johannes Lingelbach (no. 63); and two genre scenes by Isaack and Adriaen van Ostade (nos. 32 and 49). Five of these (and most of his other pictures) were purchased through the London dealer Lesser Adrian Lesser, apparently a specialist in Dutch paintings. Lesser presumably advised McEwan (who, like his daughter, always bought through dealers rather than at auction) and, judging by the quality and condition of McEwan's purchases, Lesser served his client extremely well. Other paintings bought from Lesser include two masterpieces: *The Golf Players*

by Pieter de Hooch (no. 44) and Gerard ter Borch's *An Officer making his Bow to a Lady* (no. 50).

McEwan also shared the contemporary Scottish taste for landscapes and genre scenes influenced by 17th-century Dutch painting but reinterpreted by a new generation of Dutch, Flemish and Scottish artists. In 1912 a large loan exhibition in Dundee mingled works by contemporary Dutch and Flemish artists (such as Mesdag, Mauve, Israels and Artz) with the Scottish painters whom they influenced (for example, McTaggart, Chalmers, Wingate, Bough and Graham). McEwan exhibited at least one picture at Dundee, William McTaggart's *The Pleasures of Hope* (no. 118), and owned others by him, as well as landscape and genre paintings by fellow members of the Royal Scottish Academy such as George Paul Chalmers (no. 97), and Samuel Bough (no. 92). He also bought a landscape by Anton Mauve (no. 95). The 1943 inventories of Polesden and Charles Street reveal McEwan's taste for pictures of more exotic Mediterranean and Oriental scenes by artists like Sir Ernest George and W. E. Lockhart.

It has usually been assumed that Mrs Greville's collection was compiled by advisers instructed to buy whatever was fashionable regardless of price. Certainly, the eclectic mixture of objects, from Dutch Old Masters to Fabergé trinkets, from the arts of Byzantium to those of the French 18th century, was typical of contemporary taste. Mrs Greville often paid high prices (the British portrait groups in the Dining Room, for example, were at a premium when acquired between 1917 and 1919), but she could afford to be extravagant. Apart from a little leather notebook entitled 'My Pictures', in which she drew up cryptic lists towards the end of her life, there are no personal records of her purchases or of her preferences. What she liked and why she collected have to be deduced from other

The Card Players; by David Teniers the Younger (no. 59; Picture Corridor)

sources and from the evidence of the collection itself.

In his obituary tribute in *The Times*, Osbert Sitwell declared that 'she was very fond of pictures and objects of art', although Beverley Nichols thought her 'taste in pictures was by no means impeccable'. Her career, both as a hostess and as a collector, was a very long one but, while she was susceptible to changing fashions in entertaining, she remained loyal to the *goût Duveen* in collecting. Joseph Duveen·was the most famous of the dealers who made fortunes by converting British and continental heirlooms into dollars. 'One can only say again – How utterly *duveen*,' declared Lytton

Strachey to Osbert Sitwell apropos a social *faux pas* committed by Duveen, but the epithet could equally have been applied to the collections, very similar to Mrs Greville's, that he put together for his largely American clientele, whose houses would also be built and decorated with his advice. His speciality was pictures (both British portraits and Old Masters – the Italian paintings were often acquired on the advice of Bernard Berenson, the most famous expert of the day), but he bought and sold much else, from furniture and porcelain to tapestries and sculpture. With the possible exception of a pair of French commodes (see p. 31), nothing at Polesden is known to have come from

(Right) The Golf Players; by Pieter de Hooch (no. 44; Picture Corridor)

Duveen, but some of Mrs Greville's friends (including Edward VII, George V and Queen Mary) were close to him, and it was through Duveen that Charles Allom undertook the interior decoration and arrangement of Henry Clay Frick's New York mansion (now the Frick Collection).

If Duveen can be accounted only a presiding spirit at Polesden, there is no question about the involvement of several other dealers and artistic luminaries. Mrs Greville remained loyal to Agnew's, from whom her father had bought two Dutch pictures. Between 1917 and 1940, she bought sixteen pictures from the firm (three British, one French, two German, seven Dutch, two Italian, one early Netherlandish). The three British pictures were the most expensive that Mrs Greville (or indeed her father) ever bought: Reynolds's *Nymph and Piping Boy* (no. 9) in 1917 for £7,410, and in 1918 Lawrence's *The Masters Pattisson* (no. 11) for £12,000, and Raeburn's *The Paterson Children* (no. 7) for an astonishing £23,000. Her father had

The Masters Pattisson; by Sir Thomas Lawrence (no. 11; Dining Room)

bought Raeburn's beautiful portrait of *Mrs Simpson* (no. 6) in 1896 for £2,500, and a male portrait the following year (no. 10), while Mrs Greville added his *George and Maria Stewart as Children* (no. 8; £5,500 from Colnaghi's in 1919). The outlay of £47,910 assuaged her taste for British pictures. After 1919 she bought no more, concentrating on cheaper Old Masters.

Her first purchase of an Old Master painting (and indeed her earliest recorded acquisition) was by the Genoese seicento painter Bernardo Strozzi (*A Venetian Gentleman*, no. 47), for which she paid the restorer and dealer Horace Buttery the comparatively modest sum of £650 in 1916. In 1919 and 1920 she bought nine Dutch 17th-century portraits and landscapes from Agnew's and Colnaghi's, including Frans van Mieris's minutely painted self-portrait (no. 60), which ranged in price from £750 to £3,000. The next group of three pictures was bought at Sotheby's in 1922, presumably at Mrs Greville's behest, by Tancred Borenius, a prolific Finnish art historian, Professor at University College, London, archaeologist and dealer, whose name regularly appears in the Polesden visitors' book from 1919 onwards. Borenius was well qualified to advise Mrs Greville not only on the acquisition of pictures but also of Italian maiolica. According to Kenneth Clark, who in the mid-1930s visited Mrs Greville once a week, Borenius would have been an ideal candidate for the Surveyorship of the King's Pictures (which fell vacant in 1934):

> He was a good scholar, a pleasant companion and a passionate upholder of the concept of monarchy [which must have endeared him to Mrs Greville]. He would have made an ideal courtier. Unfortunately, he was known to have followed the continental practice ... of taking payment for certificates of authenticity; and what was worse, quite small payments (known as 'smackers under the table'); if he had taken large payments, like a few scholars on the Continent, no one would have objected.

Borenius advised Mrs Greville on 17th-century Dutch pictures, but his expertise seems to have been most relevant to the important group of early Italian pictures at Polesden, which she concentrated on buying in the 1930s. The predella panel of *c.*1475 attributed to Perugino, *The Miracle of the Founding*

The Miracle of the Founding of Santa Maria Maggiore;
attributed to Pietro Perugino (no. 20; Picture Corridor)

of *Santa Maria Maggiore* (no. 20), was bought via
Borenius from Charles Langton Douglas for £600.
Langton Douglas was a multi-faceted character: ex-
Anglican chaplain in Siena, army captain, expert on
quattrocento Sienese painting, joint-editor of the
Burlington Magazine at its inception in 1903, and a
bitter rival of Bernard Berenson. Like Borenius and
Berenson, he was one of the first scholars to profit
from what Professor Ernest Samuels has called 'the
growth of the "cult of authenticity" among rich
collectors and the rise of the profession of "consult-
ing art historian"'. By the late 1920s and 1930s (the
most likely period of Mrs Greville's collecting of
Italian primitives), Douglas was based in London.
Two other pictures are known to have been
connected with him: *The Adoration of the Magi* by
the workshop of Bartolo di Fredi (no. 19), and an
early Netherlandish *Nativity* (no. 62), both acquired
by Mrs Greville in the 1930s.

Mrs Greville also acquired Italian maiolica during
the 1930s. However, given that Henry Harris, one
of her oldest friends, was a considerable enthusiast,
she may well have established her interest in
maiolica (the tin-glazed earthenware of the Italian
Renaissance) much earlier. Henry 'Bogey' Harris
was often at Polesden and Charles Street from 1908,

and must have been friendly with the Grevilles long
before. Kenneth Clark recalled that, as a fashionable, rich and handsome young man, 'Bogey' was
'sucked into the Marlborough House set. He
became friends with the Prince of Wales, and
inevitably (I am sure very reluctantly) had to play
baccarat with him. In a short time the greater part
of his patrimony had vanished.' He then went to
Italy where, under the influence of Sir Herbert
Horne (whose collection at the Palazzo Corsi in
Florence now forms the Museo Horne), he made 'a
collection of Italian art which, when installed in his
house at Bedford Square', delighted the connoisseurs and was ignored (according to Kenneth
Clark) by his society friends 'who came to play
bridge with him in spite of the religious pictures,
marble reliefs, bronzes and majolica'. Mrs Greville
was also a noted bridge player and had much else in
common with him: he was a Scot ('I hate waste. I'm
Scotch you see') and was fond of people as well as of
objects. Unlike Mrs Greville, 'he was the least snobbish of men', but he was also 'a wit, and his
comments had more sting than people realised till
they got home'. Bogey loved Mrs Greville and,
according to Clark, used to say 'one can live without everyone really; everyone but Maggie; she's
like dram drinking'.

Harris's influence on Mrs Greville's collecting
can only be guessed at, but it is not impossible that

he had the greatest (as well as the longest) influence upon her. Given that Borenius published the catalogue of Harris's maiolica collection in 1930, from which five plates later found their way to Polesden (nos. 25, 26, 27, 28 and 35), it is probable that Harris introduced Borenius to Mrs Greville around 1919, when Borenius's name first appeared in her visitors' book. In 1925 Borenius bought eight pieces of maiolica now at Polesden (nos. 22, 24, 30–33, 248 and 256) in the sale at Christie's of the celebrated collection made by Sir Francis Cook. Among these

pieces are three immensely rare figures of hawks or parrots made in mid-16th-century Urbino (nos. 30–32), for which he paid £110 5s.

Why did Mrs Greville collect Italian maiolica? It formed part of the much more extensive and famous collections of Italian art created by Sir Francis Cook (in Cadogan Square and Richmond) and Sir Julius Wernher (in Piccadilly and at Luton Hoo, Bedfordshire). However, J. V. G. Mallet has suggested that 'it was not Mrs Greville's aim to form a representative collection of the ware, but rather to

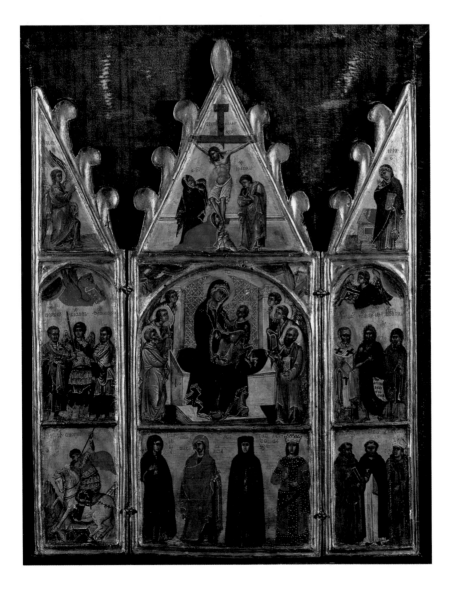

The Virgin and Child enthroned with Saints; Byzantine, first half of the 14th century (no. 21; Picture Corridor)

put together in a cabinet an attractive and decorative *ensemble*'. As he says, she bought similar pieces to make up pairs for a symmetrical arrangement: eg the Deruta plates (nos. 19a, b) and the Faenza plates (nos. 33, 34). He concludes that 'Polesden Lacey contains a number of pieces which would attract attention on their own merits in any company. Moreover, the collection never falls below a comparatively high level.'

In keeping with the maiolica is a small collection of 16th- and 17th-century French and Italian bronze statuettes which was split between Polesden and Charles Street. Some are after the Antique, but the best are from the circle of Giambologna with two early 17th-century horses in the style of Francesco Fanelli, a Florentine who worked for Charles I.

Unfortunately, it is not clear how Mrs Greville arranged her early Italian, French and Netherlandish pictures, her maiolica and her bronzes. It is possible that they were grouped together with the 16th-century French carved chairs and tables after designs by Jacques Androuet du Cerceau, and her elaborate 17th-century Franco-Flemish cabinet, in the manner of other antiquarianising high Victorian and Edwardian collections both in Europe and America. (This is how they were rearranged in 1997 in the south-west arm of the Picture Corridor.) Given that the decoration and contents of Charles Street seem to have been predominantly Louis XVI, the most likely setting would indeed have been the 'Jacobean' Picture Corridor at Polesden Lacey, where the early French and Flemish furniture was certainly listed in 1943, together with a plethora of heavy 17th-century continental furniture, most of which was subsequently sold. Most of the best pictures, the 18th-century French furniture and (probably) the best objects of vertu and jewellery were kept in London during Mrs Greville's lifetime. Her will provided for 'the pictures and objects d'art' at Charles Street to be 'taken to Polesden Lacey and added to those already there ... so as to form a Picture and Art Gallery in a suitable part of parts of the house'. Displaying the cream of one's collection in the capital was common practice at the time (a tradition deriving from the early 17th century).

Curiously, none of Mrs Greville's guests (includ-

The Judgement of Paris; maiolica dish, Castel Durante, c.1524–6 (Staircase Landing)

ing Kenneth Clark) seems to have commented on either her collection or its display. The diarist Chips Channon described Polesden in 1939 as 'full of rare china and expensive treasures', the china including a huge amount of Chinese and Japanese porcelain, which reflects Mrs Greville's taste for the Far Eastern decorative arts and chinoiserie. Her collection is distinctive both for the wealth of figures and groups and of decorative porcelain, mainly Chinese of the 17th and 18th centuries in blue and white, *famille rose*, *verte* and *noire*, and *wucai* (or five colours). Even after much of the porcelain had been packed up during the Second World War, a considerable amount remained *in situ*, notably the blue-and-white Kangxi (1662–1722) porcelain, which still remains above the bookcases in the Library. Blue-and-white porcelain, which first came into England in large quantities in the late 17th century during the north European craze for massed displays of china, was rediscovered by the aesthetes of the 1870s. The collecting of oriental porcelain then became increasingly popular and more discriminating, as connoisseurship was brought to bear on the earlier Far Eastern wares by great scholar-collectors such as George Eumorforpolos and Percival David. Unlike them, Mrs Greville's interest was focused on decorative groups and garnitures. Her taste for Chinese figures and groups of men, animals and birds was typical of the time (cf. the Gubbay collection at Clandon) and complemented her liking for European porcelain figures (mid-18th-century Meissen and the English equivalents). Porcelain at Polesden and in London was either on open display (on chimneypieces, shelves, stands or furniture) or in showcases, sometimes plain (eg the metal-framed case in the Picture Corridor) or, more usually, in 18th- or early-19th-century French style (eg Saloon). Without exception, they had glass shelves (so the marks could be seen from below) and mirrored backs.

Mrs Greville made a much smaller but none the less choice collection of late 17th- and 18th-century English silver, some of it decorated with chinoiserie engraving. Again, this was *de rigueur* for Edwardian collectors who, as Michael Clayton has pointed out, were on the lookout 'for the somewhat *outré*, and in the realm of silver their choice was that style described as *chinoiserie*, not the true *chinois* style, but that which was evocative ... of the still almost fabulous Cathay'. Between 1675 and 1690, traditional forms of English silver (eg tankards, mugs and porringers) were 'chased with figures of supposedly Oriental men strutting amid landscapes peopled with birds and foliage'. Unfortunately, once the style became sought-after at the beginning of this century, fake chinoiserie chasing was applied to otherwise genuine pieces. The Polesden collection contains examples of both high-quality original and spurious engraving (which is extremely difficult to detect). Most of the early English silver is now shown in Boulle display cabinets in the Dining Room, but it was also used by Mrs Greville to enhance the grandeur of her dining-table, which was 'laden with Georgian silver', as the *News Chronicle* remarked in 1933. Also in use (apart from a host of flatware and utilitarian silver no longer at Polesden) would have been the cake baskets by John Luff (1741) and by Phillips Garden (1750), as well as silver teapots and caddies (Tea Room).

Mrs Greville also shared contemporary collectors' liking for *objets d'art* and jewellery. Of the former, several were the gift of Edward VII and incorporate his cipher, many are by Fabergé (a taste

Several of the precious objects on display in the Saloon were gifts to Mrs Greville from Edward VII and bear his cipher

introduced into England by the Russian Imperial family and particularly by Mrs Greville's close friends, the Grand Duke Michael and his morganatic wife, the Countess de Torby), others are 18th-century French and German (snuffboxes and the like). As with her porcelain, there were numerous showcases to display them, both in her private sanctum (the 'Chippendale' bedroom suite at Polesden) and in the public rooms. As today, objects were sometimes grouped together both by category – there was a separate showcase lined with red damask for her portrait miniatures, for example – and in imaginative groupings, which was a favourite pastime of Sir Julius Wernher, whose statement 'Every vitrine must be like a picture' could equally have been made by Mrs Greville. Mrs Greville's jewels were spectacular, but although they included Marie-Antoinette's diamond necklace and the Empress Josephine's diamonds and emeralds, they were more notable for their high value than their historical associations. Mrs Greville bought jewellery to wear, in an era when hostesses 'revelled in personal splendour' and their guests were 'weighed down with jewellery'. In 1930s New York at one of Joseph Duveen's dinner parties, Kenneth Clark noted that the ladies 'even brought pieces of jewellery in their hands and laid them down on the dinner table. This could have happened in the Middle Ages.' Mrs Greville would have found this ineffably vulgar, but she had no qualms about wearing as many jewels as possible. Seeing that a rival had appeared with four strings of pearls, she rummaged in her *embonpoint* and brought her own total up to six strings: her pearl necklace was one of the finest in the world. Only Americans seem to have outshone her. Once, after dinner, Beverley Nichols remembered that 'a very rich and famous American lady discovered that the principal diamond had dropped from her necklace. It must have been about the size of a broad-bean. We all got to our knees and routed around, and then Maggie's voice was heard, speaking to a footman. "Perhaps this", she was saying, "might be of some assistance." She was handing him a large magnifying glass.' Her rubies and diamonds were equally famous: the 'fabulous diamonds still sparkled' on her hands just before her death in 1942 (one of the diamond rings had belonged to Catherine the Great). The whole magnificent collection was bequeathed to the Queen (the present Queen Mother), who wore the Greville jewels at her 80th birthday celebrations in 1980. Barbara Cartland observed maliciously that it 'must have given [Mrs Greville] great satisfaction to know that the magnificent pearls and diamonds she had worn around her fat thick neck now kept such exalted company'.

Her taste in furniture was predominantly continental, and there are only a few high-quality pieces of 18th-century English furniture, such as the lacquer commode in the style of Pierre Langlois, *c.*1760–5, in the Dining Room. This was typical of several other Edwardian collectors in Mrs Greville's orbit (Sir Julius Wernher again springs to mind). The modern comfortable or practical furniture that she placed alongside antiques – such as the Italianate easy chairs once in the Saloon and the Louis XVI-style chairs supplied through Mewès and Davis – was also mainly continental in style. Among the French furniture are several good lacquer and marquetry pieces with gilt mounts (mainly in the Saloon) stamped by prominent makers. These flamboyant commodes, secretaires and writing-tables are complemented by Louis XIV, XV and XVI seat furniture with contemporary tapestry or needlework upholstery (the marriage between chair and upholstery usually being arranged by dealers). The quality and condition of the upholstery was clearly important to Mrs Greville, whose enthusiasm for fine textiles (including Flemish tapestries) was shared by, for example, Queen Mary and Mrs Gubbay. The unusual group of French, Italian and Anglo-Dutch walnut armchairs, *c.*1680–5, in the Library is covered in nearly pristine contemporary needlework of figurative and partially chinoiserie scenes. There are also several embroidered fire-screens and even a glazed table-top set with embroidery (Central Hall), as well as three sets of mid-18th-century French walnut seat furniture covered in *gros point* embroidery (Central Hall and Picture Corridor), all of which contributed to the sense of prolific luxury, which is the essence of the Edwardian interior.

Late 16th-century gilded and engraved fretwork on the Franco-Flemish cabinet in the Picture Corridor

MRS GREVILLE AS A HOSTESS

The collections at both Polesden and Charles Street provided a *mise-en-scène* for lavish and frequent entertainments. Between June and August, and less frequently at other times, there were often dinner parties in town and a full house for 'Fridays to Mondays' at Polesden. Ronnie Greville's premature death at the age of 43 in 1908, after an operation for cancer of the throat, deprived Mrs Greville of a beloved husband, but then, as Kenneth Clark pointed out apropos Sibyl Colefax, a husband 'is always a drawback for a hostess'. Had he lived, he would have succeeded his father in 1909 as 3rd Lord Greville of Clonyn, and inherited Clonyn Castle,

Co. Westmeath, and 18,698 acres in Ireland (and another 1,178 in Kent) valued at £18,194 per annum. This potential inheritance and peerage must have made Ronnie Greville worthier of his wife's money in Mr McEwan's eyes. But Mrs Greville she remained, and with her father's death in 1913, the stage was set for her long, individual and legendary career as a hostess, collector and woman of business.

In London, she moved a few doors down from 11 to 16 Charles Street, commissioning Mewès and Davis to remodel the interior and, in the process, to install '18 carat gold scroll work in its drawing room'. Her progress as 'a charming hostess' and

The Polesden butlers and footmen, around 1928. Bole is standing on the far left, Bacon second from the right

The Dining Room table is laid for a dinner held on 25 June 1932. Mrs Greville insisted on French cuisine of the highest standard

'one of the most universally popular women in London' (as the *Onlooker* explained to its readers in 1912) can be charted in the collection of newspaper and magazine cuttings which she assiduously compiled between 1905 and 1942, in the memorabilia at Polesden, and in the diaries and reminiscences of her friends and enemies.

In the role of hostess, Mrs Greville found her true *métier*, and achieved a rare distinction. The 'browsing and sluicing', as P. G. Wodehouse put it, were of the first water – something that both guests and staff took advantage of, as Kenneth Clark recalled:

I remember one lunch [at Charles Street] with pleasure. Mrs Greville had two butlers, named Boles [in fact Bole] and Bacon. Boles looked and behaved like a butler, and fell heir to a large part of her fortune [actually, a legacy of £1,000; £500 p.a. for life and the 'modern household silver']. Bacon claimed (and no wonder) to be a communist. He was a short, stout, red-faced man who obviously put away all the drink left over by the guests. Mrs Greville's admirable cuisine was famous for one speciality, baby tongues [presumably lambs' tongues]. They were produced only for royalty. At the lunch in question I was sitting at the very end of the table, so could see round the screen that hid the serving hatch. When the baby tongues came up I saw Bacon looking at them with insuperable longing; he swayed backwards and forwards in his desire. Finally he could contain himself no longer. He stretched out his hands and began cramming the baby tongues into his mouth. The sauce ran down his shirt front, his jaws worked furiously. During the hiatus Mrs Greville said 'Boles, what's become of the baby tongues?' 'There were none to be had in the market this morning, Madam.' I expect she guessed. Bacon, his face purple with gratified desire, put a napkin over his shirt, and carried in the next course.

Even allowing for the poetic licence of this reminiscence (the butler in Oscar Wilde's *The Importance of being Earnest* uses almost identical words to cover up for his master's consumption of Lady Bracknell's cucumber sandwiches), Mrs Greville's favourite staff were undoubtedly granted the maximum of rope by their otherwise exacting mistress. Their dipsomania was well-known. On an even more famous occasion, this time at Polesden, Mrs Greville 'noticed that the butler was swaying ominously at the other end of the room [and] she wrote on a scrap of paper "You are drunk; leave the room at once", and gave the note to the footman to pass to the offender. When the butler read the message he put the piece of paper on the salver, staggered across the room and presented it to Sir Austen Chamberlain.' It was presumably Bacon who excelled himself once more at a grand dinner party in honour of Princess Juliana of the Netherlands, remembered by the 9th Earl of Portsmouth:

Mrs Ronnie had two butlers, one quite impeccable for presence and dignity; the other was equally grand but rubicund of face and egg-shaped in body. Osbert Sitwell called him Humpty Dumpty. As we were waiting for dinner, Sitwell said to me, *sotto voce*, 'I think H.D. has had one too many tonight.' We sat down about twenty-five strong at a long table laden with exotic fruits and lovely glass. When a very recherché form of fowl was before us, Humpty Dumpty served a silver dish of pillow-like *pommes gaufrettes* to Mrs Ronnie. I was heavily engulfed in conversation with Lady Simon on the evils of Chinese slavery, her pet subject, and my mind was straying with my eye about the dinner-table. Bending low over our hostess with the potatoes Humpty Dumpty belched with thunder. The explosion sent the *pommes gaufrettes* into Mrs Ronnie's hair, on to Princess Juliana's lap, into my champagne and irretrievably into the magnificent centrepiece of hothouse grapes, pears and pineapples. There was a well-bred hush, but not before I, the youngest there, had broken into a nervous yokel's guffaw. After the ladies had left us to the port, Lord Athlone, a kind and human person, said to me over his starred and beribboned shirt-front, 'My dear chap, I am glad you laughed, it saved me from apoplexy.'

Although surprisingly tolerant of such lapses, her standards were uncompromisingly high. The

The guest list and menu for a Polesden house party in June 1932

cuisine, French of course, was 'unsurpassed anywhere' (according to the *Daily Telegraph* in 1930) and was worthy of the finest productions of Anatole (the supreme chef of Bertie Wooster's Aunt Dahlia). The contents of the wine cellars at Polesden and Charles Street fetched the enormous sum of £12,600, even in 1943: there were no fewer than 500 bottles of Mrs Greville's favourite champagnes, Veuve Clicquot and Bollinger ('extra quality, extra dry'), as well as superb claret, burgundy, hock, port, sherry and brandy. The kitchens were well equipped but run on traditional lines – solid fuel only and *batteries de cuisine*. Osbert Sitwell's account of Mrs Greville's kindness to his own cook, who had been ill, struck him as typical of her 'special understanding of character':

Would Mrs Powell, she asked, care to spend the evening of the following day in the kitchen at 16 Charles Street, watching the celebrated French chef who was in charge there cook and dish up for a dinner party of some forty people? Mrs Powell accepted the invitation with rapture, and it was my opinion that the enjoyment she derived from, and interest she took in, all she saw on that occasion benefited her health more than would a whole month spent by the seaside. She returned at about midnight, in an entranced condition at the splendour of the batteries, the china, the service.

The chef's specialities included the mysterious 'Oeufs Duc de York', presumably concocted for the future George VI. If Mrs Greville discovered an unusual dish 'when she dined out at the Ritz or the Savoy or some such place', she sent her cook 'to learn the method, so there began a collection of ideas about what was good food and how to prepare it'. Beverley Nichols remembered that at Polesden tea was at 5 o'clock:

and not 5 minutes past.... Since we have already eaten a very large lunch and will shortly be eating a very large dinner ... it might be supposed that few of the guests would have much appetite for these delicacies, but they present so alluring an appearance that they are eagerly devoured.... Maggie's teas were terrific, with great Georgian teapots and Indian or China, and muffins and cream cakes and silver kettles sending up their steam, and Queen Mary saying 'Indian, if you please, and no sugar...'.

In 1936 she held her first cocktail party (for 300–400 guests), having 'previously held out against this modern form of hospitality'.

Above all, hers was a political salon, as Kenneth Clark realised: 'She was immensely rich and the only hostess who had any political power, not simply on account of her wealth, but because she was a shrewd and forceful personality. After lunch or dinner, she sat back in a large chair, like a Phoenician goddess, while the cabinet minister or ambassador leant forward attentively.' Another guest, Robert Hichens, was also struck by her acuteness:

There was a perpetual light of shrewdness in her far-seeing eyes, and she could sum up a man's character

(Right) 16 Charles Street, Mayfair – Mrs Greville's London home

more swiftly and more acutely than almost anyone else I knew. I say 'a man's character' because with me she talked more often about men than women. She was specially interested in people who had careers, who were making history, who were doing big things in one of the arts ... she now and then used her influence in high quarters to interfere in the careers of men who she was convinced were doing harm to the reputation of their country by their activities abroad.

Lord Boothby agreed that her patronage was extremely powerful, and, according to Beverley Nichols:

Her capacity for intrigue was limitless: about the time I met her there was much speculation as to who would be the next Viceroy of India and it was generally considered that Lord Lloyd, who had greatly distinguished himself in Egypt, was the most likely candidate. Maggie thought otherwise. Although he might have shone in Egypt, he had certainly failed to shine at Polesden.... She had set him at the bridge table in a foursome which included the Queen of Spain who had rashly gone a grand slam in spades. Lord Lloyd had promptly doubled her; she had redoubled; and the result, for Spain, was disastrous. All very tiresome and the man, obviously, was not quite a gentleman. I can still hear her voice as she later described to me the outcome of this unfortunate incident. 'There was a time', she purred, 'when George Lloyd thought he might get India. But I soon put a stop to that'.

Perhaps, in her view, no one could replace in that capacity three of her other guests, the great Lord Curzon, the Marquess of Willingdon and the Marquess of Reading, with whom she stayed in India in 1921–2 during the Prince of Wales's Indian tour.

Her knowledge of foreign affairs was increased by her extensive travels, not only to fashionable resorts such as Monte Carlo, Biarritz or Cannes, but also, as Osbert Sitwell pointed out, through Africa, Asia and America, where 'her eye was as observant as it was at home, and she could foretell who would be the coming figures in the countries she visited. As a result, her advice was most valuable, and she was consulted by many people of importance, and played thus a considerable part behind the scenes.' The diplomat Sir Robert Bruce-Lockhart recalled: 'Her vanity is inordinate. In those countries where she is not given a special train, the local British Ambassador or Minister gets sacked.' To the British Ambassador in Spain she wrote: 'If I were in power I would *clear out* some of the permanent officials at the Foreign Office.' As Brian Masters concluded: 'It is no wonder that European heads of state formed the impression that Mrs Ronnie Greville was an extremely important woman, a fact that was to cause much mischief as the Second World War approached.'

She was often called 'the power behind the throne' and one day told Kenneth Clark that 'during the morning three kings had been sitting on her bed'. Like Louis XIV, she was fond of *levées*,

Edward VII's bed in the King's Bedroom (not on show), as prepared for the Duke and Duchess of York's honeymoon

The Duke and Duchess of York (later George VI and Queen Elizabeth) on their honeymoon at Polesden in April 1923

even holding a board meeting of McEwan's brewery in her bedroom at Polesden one weekend in the 1930s. Afterwards, Kenneth Clark saw 'the directors leaving her room after the meeting in a very chastened frame of mind, some actually trembling'. Even allowing for a degree of snobbery, it is clear that her love of the British royal family was genuinely based upon friendship. In 1937 Harold Nicolson tried to draw her on the subject of King Edward VII: 'But she merely says that he was the only one of the family with whom she was never intimate.' This may have been discretion, but of course Edward VII was a particular friend of her husband's. Queen Mary, consort of George V, with whom she shared an interest in works of art, would often 'suddenly telephone and announce herself for tea. These were the only occasions when Maggie, who was fundamentally a very honest woman, would allow herself a little feminine conceit. She would pretend to be annoyed. "Dear Queen Mary", she would sigh, "Such a wonderful woman! But always such short notice."'

Beverley Nichols also noted that her nearest royal friends were the Duke and Duchess of York (later George VI and Queen Elizabeth): 'She once said to me that if she had ever had a daughter she would have wished her to be like the Queen Mother,' who, on returning from a state visit to Paris when Queen, had heard that Mrs Greville was ill and had immediately 'come round to Charles Street and sat by her bedside and told her all about the wonderful fairy-like time she had spent in Paris . . . and then Maggie broke off and began to cry, and said "Oh, . . . what it would be to have a daughter like that." After which, ashamed of her display of emotion – for it was her policy to emphasise her worldliness – she sat up abruptly and ordered half a bottle of champagne, and was very rude to the footman who brought it.' In 1937 Mrs Greville told Harold Nicolson that she regretted George VI's accession to the throne: 'I was so happy in the days when they used to run in and out of my house as if they were my own children.' The ultimate accolade was the Yorks' acceptance of her invitation to spend part of their honeymoon (26 April–7 May 1923) at Polesden Lacey.

The visitors' book testifies to the exclusivity of her gatherings, as Brian Masters described: 'Weekends at Polesden Lacey generally catered for about fourteen, and dinners at Charles Street were

Mrs Greville with Rip on the south terrace in July 1926

her foreign guests.' Her Indian progress in 1921–2 is charted in a photograph album which shows that she was fêted in every city, inspected troops with the Viceroy, and even had the *placement* altered at the Nizam of Hyderabad's banquet so that she could sit next to a maharaja and, more importantly, opposite the Prince of Wales. On 13 December 1921, in Calcutta, the Vicereine noted in her diary: 'Mrs Ronnie Greville arrived yesterday, very moist, *very* chatty and a game sportsman as she only arrived at 5.30 and sat down with us (100) to dinner at 8.15.' Other surviving albums cover Australia and New Zealand (1927) and South America (1924–5), where she again coincided with the Prince of Wales, and was photographed with her hired servants in her private rail carriage at 14,000 feet in the Peruvian mountains. In Hollywood, she was photographed between Spencer Tracy and Wendy Barrie.

In the 1930s, two great questions split Society: the rise of Nazi Germany and the Abdication Crisis. Kenneth Clark described Mrs Greville as the queen of a pro-Nazi circle that was 'rich – and most members of the government were rich – and who closed their eyes to Hitler [who became German Chancellor in 1933] because they, mistakenly, supposed that the Nazis were less likely to take away their money than the Bolshies [Bolsheviks].' Her appeasement line was shared by many others, and was government policy until the Nazi occupation of Czechoslovakia in March 1939, but such was her apparent influence that her views attracted particular criticism from her opponents, many of whom, like Harold Nicolson and Winston Churchill, continued none the less to partake of her hospitality. In 1936 Nicolson lunched with 'dear wee Maggie' after a long break – 'Oh, dear Harold, how you do drop your old friends' – and found himself seated 'next to a German woman who tried a little Nazi propaganda':

Poor wretch she did not know that she had a tiger lurking beside her. 'Do you know my country, sir?', she said. 'Yes I have often visited Germany.' 'Have you been there recently since our movement?' 'No, except for an hour at Munich, I have not visited Germany since 1930.' 'Oh, but you should come now. You would find it all so changed.' 'Yes I should find all my

attended by anything from ten to sixty people. There is an evening when, of sixty-one names mentioned, over fifty are titled, and many others when the guest of honour was a King, and of the thirteen other guests, ten were themselves royals.' The roll-call of her political guests was equally impressive. Prime ministers, chancellors, foreign secretaries, other high officers of state, viceroys, ambassadors and a host of other dignitaries both British and foreign entered the hospitable portals of Charles Street and Polesden Lacey.

Her gatherings were often cosmopolitan. As Lord Winterton remembered: 'She was a great traveller and, unlike some who accept hospitality from foreigners and never return it, made a point of inviting all who entertained her to stay with her in England. She always took particular pains to collect an interesting party of her English friends to meet old friends either in prison, or exiled, or murdered.' At which she gasped like a fish. Maggie saw that something awful had happened and shouted down the table to find out what it was. In a slow strong voice I repeated my remark. As Ribbentrop's Number Two was there on Maggie's right, it was all to the good.

Mrs Greville had cultivated the German ambassador, Joachim von Ribbentrop, since 1934, and was on equally good terms with Mussolini's ambassador, Count Grandi. She dangerously misled both about Britain's real views, as Nicolson recorded with disbelief in his diary in 1939:

Does Mussolini seriously suppose that he could defeat ourselves and France? Or is he still relying upon that defeatist and pampered group in London who have so long been assuring him that the capitalists of England are on his side? I do not believe that an intelligent man such as Grandi could have left him under any illusion that the will-power of this country is concentrated in Mrs Ronald Greville. He must know that in the last resort our decision is embodied, not in Mayfair or Cliveden [where Lady Astor also had a pro-Axis reputation] but in the provinces. The harm which these silly selfish hostesses do is really immense. They convey to foreign envoys the impression that policy is decided in their own drawing rooms.

Sir Robert Bruce-Lockhart noted after lunching with Sibyl Colefax in 1934 that Mrs Greville had just returned from the Nazi rally at Nuremberg full of enthusiasm for the Führer, having been treated by the Nazis as if she were royalty. Later that year, at Lady Cunard's, he sat next to Mrs Greville 'who talked pro-Hitler stuff with great vigour. She is a convinced pro-German and is very angry that no-one from the British embassy went to the Partei-Tag at Nuremberg. After all, the British Ambassador in Moscow attends the May 1 and November 7 celebrations in Moscow'. Barbara Cartland remembered that Mrs Greville spoke 'with affection' of her 'dear little brownshirts', but that her 'stream of indiscretion, innuendo and scandal' did not spare Hitler, even if he 'got a little protection because he was Head of State'.

Her Nazi sympathies are in retrospect the ugliest aspect of Mrs Greville's character, but they should be seen in the context of her times. More than one of her friends commented on her 'strong' and 'ardent' patriotism, which, as Beverley Nichols explained, 'really meant that she rejoiced in the amount of red blotches with which our early Empire builders had spattered the maps of the

The Dogs' Cemetery

world'. However, as late as 1941 she was critical of Winston Churchill in a 'heart-breaking remark', made to 'Chips' Channon: 'If only the Prime Minister could have permanent laryngitis we might win the war.' On the last time that Beverley Nichols saw her, she was in bed in her suite at the Dorchester:

[She] looked frail and shrunken, and yet indomitably *mondaine*. All the apparatus of luxury surrounded her. By her bedside was a bowl of yellow orchids.... Suddenly the windows rattled as a bomb fell unpleasantly close in Hyde Park.

'That damned Ribbentrop,' she whispered, 'Thank God I told him what I thought of him when he came to Polesden.'
'What was that Maggie?'
'I told him that if ever there was a war, he might beat the English, but he would never beat the Scots.'

Her memorial service on 23 September 1942 was 'crowded with Ambassadors and all the usual funeral faces', according to 'Chips' Channon, who afterwards at lunch at Claridges heard much talk of Mrs Greville and her famous *mots*. When Lady Chamberlain returned from Rome in early 1940, Mrs Greville remarked: 'It is not the first time that Rome has been saved by a goose.' She dismissed the over-made-up Emerald Cunard: 'You mustn't think that I dislike little Lady Cunard, I'm always telling Queen Mary that she isn't half as bad as she is painted.' About Mrs Keppel, who was making heavy weather of her escape from France in 1940, she said: 'To hear Alice talk, you would think that she had swum the Channel, with her maid between her teeth.'

Mrs Greville inspired love and hatred in equal measure, but once the *entrée* was granted, her guests, however critical of her, returned to savour what Osbert Sitwell called 'the potency of her character', which infused 'her splendid entertainments with a sense of fun and enjoyment that rendered them more memorable even than did their magnificence, or the beauty of their setting'. After all, as Sonia Keppel realised, 'Maggie's main grace was that she was interested in people'. That she could not resist being 'vituperative about almost everyone' is not inconsistent with such an interest.

In a revealing and endearingly ingenuous aside to Harold Nicolson, another connoisseur of gossip, she confided that she hated gossip, that she hoped that there would be 'no gossip at this luncheon' and that she could not stand 'people who say unkind things about other people'. She then proceeded to indulge in a spate of malevolent tittle-tattle that was greedily lapped up by the eager diarist.

Mrs Greville felt that her comparatively humble origins gave her a wider and better understanding of people than most of her friends in high society. Like her father, she was a philanthropist, most of her charitable donations being discreetly made, and she often organised entertainments for good causes. She enjoyed continuing her father's generosity to Edinburgh University, lent her pictures to exhibitions and, as her will clearly shows, anticipated the current interest in country houses and their collections by bequeathing Polesden Lacey and most of her other property to the National Trust as one of its first such acquisitions. For someone who once famously declared 'One uses up so many red carpets in a season', and who announced, 'Everybody else leaves their money to the poor; *I* am going to leave my money to the rich', the conditions of her will are surprisingly democratic. Polesden, enriched by the 'pictures and objects d'art' then at Charles Street, was 'to be held and preserved for ever' by the Trust in memory of her father. She wished the house, gardens and park to 'be open to the public at all times and that arrangements be made for the largest number of people to have the enjoyment thereof'. Ever the hostess, she felt that provision should be made for 'a Kiosk or Kiosks in the park where refreshments can be procured'.

Judging by her reference in the will to the creation of a 'Picture and Art Gallery in a suitable part or parts of the house', or even the building of a separate gallery, 'if it is considered necessary or expedient so to do', Mrs Greville probably expected Polesden to become a rather different place. Certainly, her will did not specify that everything should be kept as it was. The Trust, with the agreement of Mrs Greville's trustees, decided to retain the most important contents (of 'museum standard') and to sell the rest. Thus all the modern bedroom furniture (apart from King Edward VII's

Mrs Greville's writing-desk in the Library

bed), all the modern or second-rate utilitarian furniture in the principal rooms and the contents of the domestic quarters were sold. This was done even though the Trust's intention, according to the minutes of the 1942 committee meeting, was broadly as it remains, to furnish 'the Polesden Lacey principal rooms as living rooms'. In retrospect, it is regrettable that only the best of Mrs Greville's collections were retained for the purpose. Today, when the Trust has embarked upon filling the gaps at great expense and has rearranged the contents to give the rooms a greater sense of their original Edwardian opulence, the words of one dissenting member of the Trust's 1942 committee ring sadly true. Sir Edgar Bonham-Carter thought that the

rooms should continue to 'illustrate the surroundings in which a rich Edwardian fashionable lady lived'. 'It is not necessary', he continued, 'that the furniture in the living rooms should be museum pieces.... The suggestion that in Country Houses the Trust can only allow "museum pieces" is of course an impossible one.... Personally I should like to see Mrs Greville's bedroom with appropriate furniture open to the public. It would add much to the human interest of the house.' Prophetic words, which strike a chord now, but which were then ahead of their time.

BIBLIOGRAPHY

Mrs Greville apparently ordered that her personal papers be destroyed after her death, and this would explain the paucity of surviving material. The archive at Polesden Lacey includes probate inventories of Polesden Lacey and Charles Street, records of her entertaining and picture collecting, photographs and photographic albums, and a voluminous collection of press cuttings covering her own activities and those of her husband and father. Ambrose Poynter's plans and drawings for Polesden (1903–5), and a series of drawn schemes for garden improvements are also at Polesden. A mass of relevant secondary and comparative documentation has recently been compiled for the Polesden archive. William McEwan's early notebooks and letters are in the Scottish Brewing Archive at Glasgow University. Drawings and accounts relevant to the 1631 house, and the mid-18th-century alterations to it, are in the Minet Library, Lambeth, and in the Bodleian Library, Oxford (North MSS). Bills for Thomas Cubitt's rebuilding of 1821–3 and accounts covering the ownership of the Bonsor family are in the possession of Sir Nicholas Bonsor, Bt. Other papers relating to the history of the Polesden estate are in the Public Record Office, and in the Surrey Record Office, Guildford.

ANON., 'Domestic Architecture: Sir Ambrose Poynter, Bart: "Polesden Lacey", Dorking', *Architectural Review*, li, 1922, pp. 202–7.

ANON., 'Hostesses at Home: The Hon. Mrs Ronald Greville at Polesden Lacey', *The Onlooker*, 5 November 1910, pp. 288–91.

ANON., 'Lent for the Honeymoon: Polesden Lacey, A Home of Sheridan', *Illustrated London News*, 28 April 1923, pp. 717–20.

BENGER, F. B., 'Polesden, Great Bookham', *Proceedings of the Leatherhead & District Local History Society*, i, no. 9, 1955, pp. 25–9.

BORENIUS, Tancred, *Catalogue of a Collection of Italian Majolica Belonging to Henry Harris*, London, 1930.

CLAYTON, M. D. G., 'Silver at Polesden Lacey', *Apollo*, May 1965, pp. 380–3.

COLERIDGE, Anthony, 'French Furniture at Polesden Lacey', *Apollo*, May 1965, pp. 353–60.

FEDDEN, Robin, 'Polesden Lacey, Surrey', *Country Life*, 5, 12 March 1948, pp. 478–81, 526–9.

HARVEY, John H., 'Polesden: the Name and the Place', *Surrey Archaeological Collections*, l, 1949, pp. 161–4.

KELLY, Linda, *Richard Brinsley Sheridan: A Life*, London, 1997.

KENWORTHY-BROWNE, John, 'Rise and Demise of a Wren Church: the Reredos from St Matthew Friday Street at Polesden Lacey', *The National Trust Year Book 1977–8*, 1978, pp. 63–74.

KEPPEL, Sonia, *Edwardian Daughter*, London, 1958.

LAING, Alastair, *In Trust for the Nation*, London, 1995.

LLOYD-WILLIAMS, Julia, ed., *Dutch Art and Scotland: A Reflection of Taste*, exh. cat., National Gallery of Scotland, Edinburgh, 1992.

LLOYD-WILLIAMS, Julia, 'Ale, Altruism and Art: The Benefactions of William McEwan', *Apollo*, May 1994, pp. 47–53.

MALLET, J. V. G., 'Maiolica at Polesden Lacey', *Apollo*, October and November 1970, March 1971, pp. 260–5, 340–5, 170–83.

MASTERS, Brian, *Great Hostesses*, London, 1982.

NICHOLS, Beverley, *All I Could Never Be: Some Recollections*, 1949, pp. 9–24.

Polesden Lacey, Surrey, London, 1971 (National Trust guidebook incorporating catalogues of the pictures by St John Gore, and of the maiolica by J. V. G. Mallet).

THOMAS, Graham, 'The Walks at Polesden Lacey', *The Field*, 21 May 1964, pp. 1006–7.